Praise for My Life with Deth

"Ellefson is the founding bass guitarist of the multimillion-copy-selling metal band Megadeth. He is also studying to be a Lutheran pastor and is the son of a Minnesota farmer. How all that hangs together—and it does—is the subject of his memoir, cowritten with English music journalist McIver. . . . Metal music fans will find this a fascinating backstage read. . . . Yet everyone can appreciate Ellefson's unpretentious tone and the delightful irony of a serious Christian who helped define seriously heavy metal music."

— *Publishers Weekly*

"An inspiring book on how a man's faith pulled him out of his addictions and put him on top again in the metal world and, more importantly, in life."
— Jim Florentine, co-host of VH1's "That Metal Show" and Sirius/XM's "Metal Midgets"

"David tells it the way it is. What makes this an enjoyable read is how honest he is with the reader. There is something very sincere in the way he opens the door to his life and walks you through some of his darkest hours. . . . What I liked most about the book is that I never once felt like Ellefson was trying to sell me a load of bull. The stories were honest as embarrassing or painful as they may have been for him."

—*Soundcrave Magazine*

MY LIFE WITH DETH

Discovering Meaning in a Life of Rock & Roll

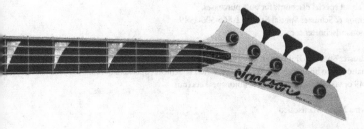

DAVID ELLEFSON

with Joel McIver

HOWARD BOOKS

A DIVISION OF SIMON & SCHUSTER, INC.

NEW YORK NASHVILLE LONDON TORONTO SYDNEY NEW DELHI

Howard Books
A Division of Simon & Schuster, Inc.
1230 Avenue of the Americas
New York, NY 10020

First Howard Books trade paperback edition July 2014

HOWARD and colophon are trademarks of Simon & Schuster, Inc.

For information about special discounts for bulk purchases,
please contact Simon & Schuster Special Sales at 1-866-506-1949
or business@simonandschuster.com.

The Simon & Schuster Speakers Bureau can bring authors to your live event.
For more information or to book an event, contact the Simon & Schuster Speakers Bureau
at 1-866-248-3049 or visit our website at www.simonspeakers.com.

Designed by Davina Mock-Maniscalco

Manufactured in the United States of America

10 9 8 7 6 5 4 3

The Library of Congress cataloged the hardcover edition as follows:

Ellefson, David
  My life with Deth / David Ellefson with Joel McIver.
    pages cm
1. Ellefson, David, 1964– 2. Megadeth (Musical group) 3. Bass guitarists—United States—Biography
4. Rock musicians—United States—Biography. 5. Heavy metal (Music)—History and criticism.
I. McIver, Joel. II. Title.
ML419.E45A3 2013
787.87′166092—dc23[B]   2013011325

ISBN 978-1-4516-9988-3
ISBN 978-1-4767-2822-3 (pbk)
ISBN 978-1-4516-9989-0 (ebook)

This book is dedicated to the Ellefson family,
past, present, and future.

Contents

Foreword

Hard rock can sometimes take people to many dark and unexpected places. David Ellefson has traveled down this rough road for many years: like many of us, he has been to hell and back.

There are sometimes immense outside expectations for rock stars to be dangerous, mysterious, and self-destructive. Some of us get through it sober, but unfortunately some of us burn out and die before our time: it's a difficult thing to endure without help.

David was able to see what was happening to himself and to those around him. He accepted that he needed help, and he is now living his life the way he wants to. Ironically, sometimes the most rebellious and controversial thing a rocker can do is become a Christian.

Alice Cooper, 2013

Introduction

At first, I didn't want to write this book. Not because I didn't want to share my life with you, but because it seems that celebrity tell-all books are in vogue and a dime a dozen these days. In fact, most of the ones I've skimmed at the bookstores begin with tragedy and go downhill from there!

Well, that is not my story—and that was not my life. Fortunately, my friend the journalist Joel McIver bugged me for more than two years to start recording my life with him via Skype while I traveled the world. I agreed to do at least this much and contacted my pastor in Scottsdale, Arizona, for some direction: he suggested that, rather than just write another tell-all tale of rock 'n' roll woe, I should consider another angle for my book—one that was a bit more truthful about my journey as a man, not only as a rock star.

He suggested that I give a testimony of my life instead, and that this book could be more than just a fascinating read: it could also be a fantastic opportunity to share with you my struggles with faith and addiction. It hit me that people everywhere need to feel inspired, and to know that they can keep their dreams alive and their faith in tow, yet still prosper in a world that tells us to bend the rules and compromise ourselves in order to win. I learned these lessons the hard way, and they—along with friendships, forgiveness, and reconciliation—are the basis of this book.

I began having casual conversations with Joel, back in his office in England, from various locations around the world. As we talked, the stories unfolded and the manuscript was born. Those conversations led to the volume in your hands. A note before you begin the first chapter: this book is not solely about Megadeth, the band I cofounded in 1983 and which has been my home for the majority of my career. It is about the lessons I have learned while in Megadeth and beyond.

I've been blessed with a good life. I have, for the most part, been spared the devastating elements of show business to which many of my contemporaries succumbed. In fact, my life is fairly normal when you consider the circus of rock 'n' roll that enveloped me during my professional years in the music business and, indeed, as far back as the age of thirteen. But hey—at least it was a fun circus!

Without further ado, let's pull back the curtains and let the show begin. . . .

David Ellefson
Scottsdale, Arizona, 2013

Prologue

What's withdrawal from heroin like? Well, it's like being very sick with the flu, while knowing that if you could just go and score, you'd be better within three to five minutes. Your stomach is upset, you're aching everywhere, and it's just plain horrible.

This was how I was feeling on August 20, 1988, as my band Megadeth was flying to England to play for 107,000 people at the renowned Monsters of Rock festival at Castle Donington. I should have been feeling on top of the world. Instead, I was in a hell of my own making.

We arrived in England and drove up to the show, about two hours north of London. I had to get rid of my smack on the plane before I arrived at Heathrow Airport immigration, and the inevitable withdrawal hit me like a punch to the stomach. I went to our hotel and became so sick that everybody found out about it. Everyone was shocked. I'd been such a good addict—so sneaky. "You junkie American!" said the doctor.

Once I got off the stage, I was so sick I just went to the bus.

It was all such a long way from where my story began. . . .

Farm Boy

"If you don't build your dream, someone will hire you to help build theirs."

—Tony Gaskins

I grew up on a farm about six miles north of Jackson, Minnesota, in a little town of about three thousand people. My very first memory, from when I was two years old or even younger, is of my grandmother holding me while I was looking out of the dining-room window, watching the cattle trucks come in and out of the yard.

Ellefson is a Norwegian name, though my combined ancestry encompasses Norway, Germany, England, Denmark, and Sweden. My paternal grandparents were Henry and Anna Ellefson. I didn't get to know them well as I was very young when they both passed away from congestive heart failure, the same illness that would claim their son, my father, many years later. I knew my mother's parents, Arthur and Isabel Jorgenson, much better and spent many weekends on their farm in Gillette Grove, Iowa, about twenty minutes southwest of Spencer.

Grandma Isabel was very strict, but Art was a funny little bald grandpa who liked the occasional girlie pinup magazine and firearms and was fascinated with the railroad. He had a terrific Winchester .22 Magnum rifle with which we would target-shoot in the pasture outside the front window of his old farmhouse. I always had great aim and good shooting technique and once even pegged a sparrow right off a telephone wire, although we were expressly forbidden to shoot in that direction because if we hit the wire itself, the house would be out of phone service for several days until the company could get out to repair the line. Once Grandpa Art saw that I was fascinated with guns, he eventually gave me that rifle as a present, which is at my brother's house to this day. In many ways, firearms were my first obsession, just before I discovered the bass guitar.

My mom, Frances, was a registered nurse and had studied nursing in North Platte, Nebraska. They had my brother, Eliot, on May 15, 1963, and I was born on November 12, 1964. My mother gave up her nursing career to raise my brother and me. She was very hands-on and very sweet and happy: the quintessential good-Samaritan church mom. She was wonderful. My father, by contrast, was very much a no-nonsense kind of man: he would flip out whenever he heard me swearing, for example. He was the stern parent, and my mother was the friendly one.

My dad was a beef farmer in the early days. He had a heart attack when I was two years old, no doubt because he smoked and because the midwestern American diet is rich in meat, so he ended up selling off the beef cattle and transitioned into grain farming. My dad was not a traditional overalls-and-pitchfork farmer: he was an astute businessman. In fact, generations of Ellefsons were astute businessmen. They were a conservative, educated, traditional pack of men.

Ours was an eleven-acre farm in the middle of a square mile of flat farmland. In fact, everywhere in Minnesota where I grew up was sectioned into square miles, with big open areas of either corn or soybean fields. It was great to grow up there because you could shoot guns, fire a bow and arrow, or drive a golf ball, and you wouldn't hit anything. We were surrounded by wide-open spaces and never had any fear of danger, kidnapping, or burglary. We would even leave our houses unlocked and the keys in our cars. Neighbors would stop by to visit over coffee with my parents for hours at a time. Life on the farm was simple and founded on industry and the strong work ethic that carved out the character of that part of the Midwest.

I was brought up Lutheran, and our family meals always began with a mandatory Lutheran prayer of "Come Lord Jesus, be our guest, let this food to us be blessed. Amen." That was the prayer, said by all in attendance; no negotiation! Meals were very much family times— morning, noon, and night.

I was not silver-spooned by any means, but by today's standards, much of my upbringing was upper middle class. When I was a small child, my family was of fairly humble means, but there was a period in the 1970s when we did quite well in the farming industry. All of a sudden we were remodeling the house and getting new furniture. Probably the biggest indicator of our newfound prosperity was when my dad built an indoor swimming pool and some new farm buildings, and we had five cars in the garage.

I remember my parents teaching me how to understand our new wealth, saying: "Hey listen, we're going to have a swimming pool. There are only one or two other families in this entire county who have a pool, so don't go to school and brag about it." They were almost warning us that this wealth could lead to us being perceived as arrogant and snotty, and we didn't want that. The truth is that farming is much like the music business, literally feast or famine, with so many elements that are beyond one's control. We were taught to continue to work hard on the farm and be humbly thankful for our blessings.

The boom in farming didn't last, though. After Ronald Reagan came into office, the Russian grain embargo was enacted, which was all part of the continuing Cold War. All of a sudden piles of surplus grain were scattered all over the Midwest, and grain prices came tumbling down.

Between 1978 and 1980, land prices were at an all-time high, and my dad went out—as a bunch of other farmers did—and took out adjustable-rate, high-interest loans, which created the landslide in the farming industry. Suddenly, high mortgages on land, coupled with falling grain prices, created a perfect storm and a lot of families lost their farms. I later chronicled this time period in Megadeth's hit song "Foreclosure of a Dream."

I loved the farm, but I didn't love farming quite so much, so my brother, Eliot, was always the one who was going to take it over from my father when the time came. He showed an aptitude for farming from a very young age. When I started getting into music at eleven or twelve, Eliot was focusing on being disciplined and working around the farm.

Because of that, my dad was comfortable letting me pursue my passion for music. My father's passion was architecture: as a young man he studied it formally for a year at the University of Minnesota before returning to take over the family farm, and he always had blueprints, plans, and drawings lying around. He built the swimming pool and remodeled the house himself, drafting it all beforehand. It was pretty impressive, looking back on it now.

My family belonged to Our Savior's Lutheran Church in Jackson. My dad became very involved in that the church, and my mother sang in the choir. Eliot and I spent our youth there, eventually receiving our Lutheran instruction and confirmation at that church. In fact, he and my mother are still members there to this day, and I visit it every time I go back between world tours.

The pastor of Our Savior's Lutheran Church, Pastor Tange, had a son named Dwight who was a longhair—not a disrespectful partier guy, just a typical '70s kid. He drove the school bus. Dwight would always listen to rock 'n' roll radio on the bus, especially WLS, which was an AM station out of Chicago, and that's when I started hearing things like Styx and their songs "Lady" and "Lorelei." I also heard the Sweet and songs like "Ballroom Blitz" and "Love Is Like Oxygen." As soon as

I heard rock 'n' roll on the bus, man, my life started to change quickly. I loved distorted guitars: I didn't know what they were, but I knew I liked them.

My dad had hired a farmhand named Gary Regnier, who had an eight-track cartridge of Bachman Turner Overdrive's *Not Fragile* album, which came out in 1974, when I was nine years old. I'd ride with him in the tractor, which was one of the first tractors to have an eight-track player and be soundproofed and air-conditioned: it was a really nice piece of machinery. I'd listen to the music and I loved it. My buddy Greg Handevidt, who eventually moved to Los Angeles with me after we graduated in 1983, had the twelve-inch gatefold LP of that BTO album. You opened it up and it had the full band photo. I remember seeing Randy Bachman with a Fender Stratocaster, Blair Thornton with a Gibson SG, and Fred Turner with a black-and-white Rickenbacker 4001 bass.

Greg Handevidt (school friend):

I first met David in sixth grade, when my family had just moved to Jackson. We were both KISS fans, and that's how we connected. I saw him in the hallway with "KISS" written on one of his books, and I said to him, "KISS uses Gibson guitars and Pearl drums," and he shot back, "And Marshall amps!" He was a popular kid; everybody liked him.

I'd never known there was such a thing as a bass guitar. The neck was long, and it had big fat strings, and it sounded different . . . and cool. Then I heard KISS. Their song "Shout It Out Loud" was so special to me: it turned my ear entirely. Gene Simmons was playing a Gibson Grabber bass guitar on the cover of KISS's *Alive* LP, and something about that instrument drew me.

Meanwhile, as I was getting into rock 'n' roll, things were starting to change a little at home on the farm. My family started to attend evening parties at some of the nearby neighbor homes. I had never known my parents to drink, and all of a sudden I'm nine or ten years old, and we're hanging with these families that drank a lot.

I remember one night coming home from a neighbor's house, and it was almost like my mom and dad were joyriding. We pulled over, and one of them opened the door and threw up on the side of the road! It was very disturbing. I was like, "This is chaos—what's going on here?" Even at a young age, I found it scary and I didn't like it. It was my first introduction to the unsettling ways of drinking and the erratic behavior that came with it.

We also started to go to concerts at the Armory in downtown Jackson, which held about a thousand people in a big dance setting. Country music bands played there, and I would always watch the bass players. I was instantly drawn to the instrument. Back at the house, we'd watch a TV show called *Hee Haw*, which was very popular. I hated the music, but I was drawn to the instruments and the flash and the showbiz; it just drew me in. I couldn't get enough of it.

My mom was cool with me getting into rock music. She sang in the church choir, but she had grown up with rock 'n' roll—she had seen Elvis play at the Veterans' Auditorium in Des Moines, Iowa. She told me that the place wasn't even full because this was right before Elvis got popular. He tossed a scarf out into the crowd, and my mom actually caught it. She recently told me that when she passes away, she wants Marty Friedman, who later played guitar in Megadeth, to have that scarf because he's the biggest Elvis fan ever.

She loves Marty and thinks the world of him. She was always cool with rock 'n' roll. She got it.

We had a cassette player in my mother's Wurlitzer organ at home, which was pretty new technology at the time. One of the tapes we used to listen to all the time was *Jesus Christ Superstar*, which I loved because it was rock. It felt dangerous, even the title. It was kind of like church, but it didn't sound like it was approved by the church.

I learned how to play music on that Wurlitzer organ, which was excruciatingly boring. Then in the fifth grade I took up the tenor saxophone, mostly because it looked like the coolest instrument in the ensemble. I later learned that women like a sax man, so I should have gotten better at it, but it just wasn't my bag. I mostly did it because I wasn't into being a jock, and I needed to take some sort of elective.

All these things led up to me asking my mom for a Gibson bass in the summer of 1976, when I was eleven years old. I wanted a Gibson because I'd seen the brand name on the back of a KISS album: I figured that if KISS used it, it must be the only one to have. Gibson had to be a go-to brand. We found a used Gibson EB-0 bass that came up for sale in the neighboring town of Fairmont, and we bought it for $150. Then we went to Worthington Music in a town about thirty miles away, and bought a little twelve-watt Fender Bassman amp with a twelve-inch speaker.

It sounded awful, believe me. That combination of a Gibson EB-0, with its single pickup at the neck, plus flatwound strings and that little amplifier was terrible, especially at the volumes I wanted to play it. I got home and plugged in and I thought, "What the heck is this? This doesn't sound like Gene Simmons at all!" I took note of this in my later career: when a kid buys one of my signature Jackson basses, I want it to sound like *Countdown to Extinction* or *Rust in Peace*. Even if the guy can't play it, just striking the strings should make the bass sound something like "Holy Wars . . . The Punishment Due."

Even though it sounded terrible, I'd come home after school every day and for many hours I'd sit in the basement and learn to play that Gibson bass.

My brother wasn't like me: he played trombone for a couple of years in the school band, but my mom and dad had to stay on him the whole time to practice. He didn't enjoy it; his musical tastes were different. He was into pop acts like Elton John and the Bay City Rollers. I didn't appreciate Elton John until years later, because I regarded the piano as a lightweight, sissy instrument, and I didn't care for it. I was into really heavy hard rock. Eliot also integrated more into the community than I did, and he started to get into country music, but music was strictly background for him.

I really diverged from the family in that sense. My parents remained supportive, but both of them were very cautious because they knew about the allure and the dangers of rock 'n' roll. I remember the father of a friend of mine telling me that I should go down to the Armory and play country music gigs, because I could make fifty bucks a week doing it. I thought, "Forget the fifty bucks. I'd rather play rock 'n' roll for free!"

I didn't want to be a working guy: I wanted to be a rock star. The '70s were such a cool time for rock 'n' roll: bell-bottoms, platform shoes, long hair, sex appeal, cool guitars, glitter, studs. It was all so attractive to a young, impressionable person like me.

So here I am in the summer of 1976, age eleven and heading toward twelve. KISS's *Destroyer* had just come out, and my number-one ambition was to be a rock 'n' roller. I had the Mel Bay *Electric Bass Method Volume 1* and *Volume 2* tuition books that I'd bought from the music store, and I basically taught myself to play bass from those books in my basement. I was so desperate to learn the instrument that at one point, I even called on one of the church music leaders, a guitar player, to come over and show me things as best he could. I would go to any lengths in small-town Minnesota to find musical camaraderie, so I could play the bass.

But I didn't want to just sit in the basement and be a great player for myself; I wanted to play in a band. I wanted to be onstage and emulate the musicians I'd seen. What's interesting is that I wasn't an extrovert or a kid who needed attention; I was actually rather shy and didn't always like being the center of attention. But the bass guitar lit me up: it was the thing that gave my life purpose and direction.

Eliot had two high school buddies, a guitarist named Mike Cushman and a drummer named Kent Libra, who were both pretty good players. We formed a band within three months of me starting to play the bass, and played covers of songs by Bachman Turner Overdrive, Kansas, KISS, and other bands, just copying what our heroes were doing. We did our first concert out on the porch of Mike's farmhouse one night, in front of all the parents. That was the first time I performed live in front of an audience in a rock 'n' roll band.

The band was called Headstone, because that was the darkest thing we could think of at that age. I wore a cool pair of black platform shoes, because I'd been watching what KISS was doing. I had some bellbottoms, too, white flashy ones, with a wine-colored satin button-up shirt. I was taking fashion cues from my idols, mostly '70s rock stars. The parents looked at me with a bit of amusement, raising their eyebrows, but I didn't care. I was gonna be a rock star, and it was all starting now.

I started to grow my hair out about this time. When I was a little kid, I killed one of my front baby teeth with a Tinkertoy and it went yellow and died. So when my permanent teeth came in they were all messed up, crooked as could be. As a result, I had to get braces at around twelve years of age, which was so not cool for a budding rock star, and I had real bad acne till I was seventeen. It was right about that time that I started to have long hair around my ears. I remember wearing that maroon silk shirt around, which I'd have open, with the buttons undone. I was starting to look at the world in the way that I thought a rock star would, even at this very young age.

My father saw me getting really into this rock star stuff, and one day we went over to a music store in Sioux Falls, South Dakota, where they had a Dan Armstrong acrylic bass guitar. It cost five hundred dollars new, and he bought it for me, so now I had a collection: my Gibson EB-0 and my new Dan Armstrong. My father didn't have a musical bone in his body, but he could tell when something had real value, and even to him this Dan Armstrong bass was something special.

This set a precedent: throughout my whole career, I've always had flashy instruments. I've never had just a standard Fender Precision bass, for example, even though I temporarily wanted one because many of the 1970s rock bassists seemed to have them. That said, at the store in Sioux Falls, they had a really old, beat-up Ampeg SVT amplifier, and I looked at it as if I was worshipping in front of an altar. Every hero of mine had an SVT, and even though this one didn't sound that good, it was an iconic piece of gear to me, through which all the arena rock gods played. However, I couldn't afford it at the time and didn't buy it, but this was a blessing in disguise because I was able to create my own individual sound. Ironically, not having the standard Fender bass plugged into an Ampeg SVT helped me to develop a unique tone. It was largely because I didn't have these tools that I was forced to develop a style that would allow me to cut through the mix. One of those was playing the bass with a pick instead of taking the typical two-finger plucking approach.

I initially learned how to play the bass with my fingers, but I found that style awkward, and once I started playing in a loud rock environment, I always felt that a pick sounded better. I could wear the bass in a different position where it felt cooler on my body, too: I never liked the look of the guys who had their bass high up so they could play with their fingers. I thought it looked effeminate, so I would play it down low and rock out with a pick. It made me feel like a rifleman going into battle, and it remains my stage stance to this day.

The first major show I saw was KISS with Uriah Heep opening on their Rock and Roll Over tour, in February 1977, when I was twelve. We all went up to Bloomington, a suburb of Minneapolis, to the Met Center, where the Minnesota North Stars played hockey. My mom and her friend Sheri took me and Eliot, his friend Mike, my friend Greg, and Sheri's daughter Marci to the show. It was amazing. I'd seen the pictures of the band and watched them on the *Paul Lynde Halloween Special* on TV, but in the arena it was a whole different experience. I just remember how enormous it was and wondering how KISS had gotten to this point. It seemed almost overwhelming, like looking at a jet airplane and wondering how in the world that thing could ever get off the ground.

I remember there being pot smoke everywhere—this was still the '70s. As the night wore on, it seemed as if everyone in the audience was smoking pot. At one point in the night, these heads in front of us turned and offered some to me and Greg, and we said, "Oh no, we don't do that!" I was completely naïve, and my mother was somewhere close by, chaperoning the trip, and she certainly would have frowned upon this. After the show I remember buying a T-shirt outside for six dollars; it fell apart after only a few washes in the washing machine. I now know that it was a bootleg shirt but when you're a young, naïve fan, you just want to take something home as a souvenir. Things in the concert business were much looser in those days than they are now.

Right about this time, Mike and Kent from my band Headstone had started to play with two other guys, Lee Meecham and Jim Tusa, both of whom were very accomplished guitar players in the area. They were about sixteen years old and went to high school, Jim in Jackson and Lee in the neighboring town of Fairmont, where I'd bought my Gibson EB-0 bass a few years earlier. They had cool gear: Electro-Harmonix Big Muff pedals, Fender Stratocasters and Gibson Les Paul copies, plus big amps. They had great licks and really looked like rock stars. Kent and another bassist, who played in our high school jazz band, came and played with these guys on a regular basis, but suddenly he couldn't do it. So Kent and Mike said, "Let's get Ellefson in!"

Here I am at thirteen, and I've joined a band with a bunch of fif-teen- and sixteen-year-olds. I was always in bands where guys were older than me, which has helped me become a much better musician. I now knew what it felt like to be brought in as the new guy, plug my gear in and play with good tone, and have people say, "Wow, this kid is a good addition to what we're doing." Every gig I've done since then, I've always wanted to be that guy: the guy who can improve the band, not take something away from it. What's more, by joining this band, I discovered that those Electro-Harmonix Big Muff pedals could make guitars distort and sound like real rock guitars, just like on the records I was listening to.

We called ourselves the River City Band, largely because Jackson had the Des Moines River running through the middle of town and it was our connection to the area. It only lasted a short time: we played a couple of school functions and that was about it. In fact, I recall getting a gig at Riverside Elementary to play for the students, and it was truly electrifying. We had lights, sound, roadies, a dressing area, stage clothes—the whole bit. But from there it was a fun summertime thing to do after I'd been playing for a year or so. As with a lot of bands, interest waned and people got sidetracked by other things, but we did play live a few times.

Another time, I remember going to Fairmont and playing a teen hall or something like that. We had to learn a lot of material and play three or four forty-five-minute sets that night, which was standard for hired-out bands in those days, in that part of the country. I liked learning about show business. You'd have a stage time, start with an intro tape, and play your set. You'd take breaks in between and then play another set. It definitely got your chops up, as well as your endurance. Usually by the end of the night I was really tired from the energy of it all, and I wouldn't get home till almost 3 A.M. I wouldn't call it rock stardom so much as just working in a rock 'n' roll band . . . usually for free, after the travel expenses ate up the band's fee.

That was one of the first times I saw musicians drinking beer at a gig, and girls coming around backstage to smoke pot and get friendly with the band. After the midshow parties at the breaks, the guys would go back onstage and their playing was terrible. I was really bummed out by this. I was like, "Why did you do that? You ruined our show!" I was in the pursuit of excellence, and because I wasn't taking part in the party life, I didn't yet understand that aspect of the rock 'n' roll lifestyle. My passion for music was all encompassing, and as a result, when I saw guys smoking pot and drinking and getting distracted by girls, I looked at them as if they were a bunch of losers.

I wasn't involved with the church much by this point. There was a disturbing period when I was around fifteen years old, when a religious group called the Peters Brothers out of Minneapolis embarked on a crusade of burning rock 'n' roll records. Their point of view was that KISS was an acronym for "Knights In Satan's Service," and that Rush was about injecting heroin, and so on: they really took the morality angle to the edge. My mom came home one night from one of their seminars in Jackson, quite shocked and obviously reconsidering everything I was listening to. That, more than anything, turned me away from the church, although my mother eventually relaxed on the whole issue.

I was becoming rebellious at this point, though. I'm sure part of it was the allure of rock 'n' roll mixed with typical teenager stuff. I remember coming home with a pierced ear and, although I kept my hair over my ear to hide it, one day we were sitting at the kitchen table and my dad looked at me with the most disapproving glare. I thought he was going to kill me. He supported me in music, but seeing his son dress the part of a rock star never really sat well with him.

Greg Handevidt and I were close friends—he was probably my best friend throughout most of my teenage school years. He had moved to Jackson in the fifth or sixth grade, and he was a troublemaker. He was always getting yelled at by the teachers, which I didn't like so much, but I liked the fact that he was into KISS and had started to play a copy of a Les Paul guitar. He had lived in bigger cities than Jackson prior to moving there, so he was cocky and had an air about him as if he knew what was going on more than the rest of us. I'd go to his house, and he'd play BTO and KISS records on his stereo. We'd watch TV if there was any kind of rock 'n' roll show on, especially *The Midnight Special*, featuring Wolfman Jack, and also *Don Kirshner's Rock*

Concert. Greg seemed to know rock history and was quite diverse in his tastes. I remember arguing with him once about what KISS wore on the Halloween TV special, which they played during the Destroyer tour, and even the details of Gene Simmons's bass at the concert we attended in Bloomington. We were passionate about rock 'n' roll and about making it big as musicians. Plus, he had a real street-smart sense about him, whereas I was pretty wholesome and naïve, being from the farm.

Greg was a mentor to me. He had lived in the city, and even though he was a few months younger than me, he was way more worldly than I was. He was into sports, which I wasn't. He would tell me, "You need to get into sports so you can get in shape." He was great when it came to teaching me not to be a dork from the farm. Pretty soon Greg and I got together with a drummer and formed a band called Toz. I have no idea what the name means, although I found out later that the fifth row down of an ophthalmologist's eye chart is made up of those letters.

Greg Handevidt (school friend):
We were going to call the band Toyz, but then we
realized how wimpy that sounded, so we dropped the y.

This is about the time I started drinking and using drugs myself. It's interesting: from the ages of fifteen to twenty-five, which were the years I participated in drugs and alcohol, the people I hung with were all defined by the chemicals they were using.

When it came to alcohol, I had been quite sheltered from it all. I'd had a couple sips of my father's beer and taken communion in church, which of course involved wine, and there were a couple of instances at Thanksgiving where I'd have a little glass of wine. I'd have that feeling of the alcohol hitting my head, and then I'd get really tired and sleepy. I liked the taste of grape juice better, so I wondered why people drank wine. I never liked the taste of alcohol, actually. Kind of ironic, considering the events that were about to happen next.

A THOUGHT

Religion: Opiate for the Masses?

I spent the early years of my life on the farm in and around the church. Nothing fanatical, but I still had the fundamentals of a Christian ideology put upon me. Years later I would philosophize and question these teachings, even though they were the basis of my upbringing.

Because of this moral compass, as a young man, I looked down my nose in disgust at older musicians who would partake of booze and drugs before we performed. I simply thought they played better when they weren't stoned. That all changed once I took my first hard drink, though, and for the next ten years of my life I sought to feel good just like they did, usually with whatever they were offering. In many ways, I left religion behind, only to get caught up in a different type of opiate for my soul.

CHAPTER TWO

One Is Too Many
(and a Thousand Isn't Enough)

"The best way to never have to quit taking drugs is to simply never start taking them."

—Donald Trump

One autumn night, I went out with my brother, Eliot, and his two friends, Mike and Todd. We sat out in Todd's car, on a dirt road about half a mile or so from where I grew up. I don't think they invited me: I was just the younger brother who tagged along for the night. I remember it was a cold fall night, probably in early September.

They had some Southern Comfort, peppermint schnapps, Miller beer, and Marlboro cigarettes—and we threw it all back and got hammered. I remember those first couple of sips of Southern Comfort were wretched: it tasted so bad. They said, "Chase it with a Miller beer!" so I did, which made it a little more tolerable, mostly because of the barley taste of the beer. The schnapps was much smoother and even helped the Comfort go down a bit easier.

All of a sudden a warm, floating, fuzzy feeling came over me, and I started giggling and laughing. I was laughing at them and they were laughing at me, and that was my formal introduction into the world of alcohol at the age of fifteen, in September 1980. We went to the bowling alley that night and played Asteroids. I thought, "Okay, so this is what stoners and drinkers do." Late into the night, Eliot and I snuck into the house while our parents slept, essentially getting away with it all.

The next day I remember waking up with a slight hangover but feeling great about the night before. It was so much fun, and my next thought was, "When are we going to do that again?" Being under the legal drinking age, which was nineteen in Minnesota at that time, I started scheming ways to find people old enough to buy booze so my buddies and I could go out drinking Friday and Saturday nights. In addition to playing in bands, partying now became my new passion.

My buddies would also go on about their sexual escapades, which I was sure were nothing but tall tales to make themselves the center of attention. Now that door was opened for me, too. Alcohol provided my first introduction to girls. I'd start to see the developing girls from my school classes attending keg parties, and suddenly we had a connection. When I was sober, I was shy around girls. But the booze became a social lubricant to help me open up all sorts of doors with them.

What was interesting is that although I had embraced the party lifestyle, one that was intriguing and fun, albeit dangerous, I could always hear the rules of my church upbringing chiming in my head, as if a voice were saying, "You'd better watch out. You know what you're doing is wrong and that you will pay for this, sooner or later."

When I was playing in my bands, I really tried to limit the drinking. I didn't want to drink before I played, because I wanted to keep the music my number-one priority. I learned later that drugs and alcohol would essentially rob me of that passion. I'd always get mad at the other guys in the band when they would drink before they went onstage, because they were buying into the sex, drugs, and rock 'n' roll ethos—whereas I was still into rock 'n' roll for its own sake.

Another time, I was out with a couple buddies from a very strict religious family. They were into cool music, though, and turned me on to more eclectic and trippy bands like the Cars and Yes. I was with them the first time I smoked marijuana. I didn't get high that first time, and I thought, "There's nothing wrong with this stuff—it must just be a psychological high." I had heard in physical education health class that some drugs provided a physical high, while others were psychological. I didn't understand it, but I thought that maybe this was what pot was. I smoked it again one night a few weeks later, on the way to a church roller-skating function. I was toking in the car, and I remember choking and coughing on the smoke, and seeds falling out and burning holes in my friends' car seats. I didn't feel anything until I stepped out of the car. It was probably during October, so it was cold outside, and I walked in the door of the roller-skating club, and all of a sudden the pot just came over me. My eyes were red; I had the munchies; I couldn't stop laughing; I was out of control. But no one died and no one went to jail, so I thought, "Well, that's safe: I'll definitely be doing that again. Add that one to the list."

Just like my first night of drinking, I kept the pot smoking hidden, as it was important to me not to be found out. This later became the routine of my drug abuse. I felt a little weird for a day or so afterward, because of the aftereffects, and also because I was lying and doing something illegal, which led to feelings of guilt and shame. It was as if I were in a secret little club at school that my parents and teachers couldn't find out about. I still thought it was all part of normal teenage life, and for many it was. But according to my upbringing, it was definitely out of line and I knew it. Drugs and alcohol were supposed to have no place in the life of a teenager.

My older brother, Eliot, didn't smoke pot, but he drank casually with his friends in town. I do remember as a teenager that he bought himself a Pontiac Trans Am for his sixteenth birthday and he was the envy of the town. I was happy because I had an older brother with cool wheels, until I woke up one morning to see his car being towed up the driveway by a tow truck because he'd crashed it the night before.

All in all, the party life was pretty fun in small-town Jackson, although every now and then I wondered if I was doing the right thing and questioned my own morals. A turning point came when I went to a keg party over on the east side of town where it wasn't so affluent. I was doing some drinking and smoking some pot with buddies in the living room. I knew the guy hosting the party was a bit of a troublemaker and not someone I would normally hang out with. He was certainly not someone with whom I had much in common, until I started getting loaded. But I had a moment of clarity while I was at his party: I realized that I was now willing to associate with people I really didn't like, because they had something I wanted—in other words, booze and pot.

I left that party with another buddy, who was driving and had just gotten his license. Almost immediately upon leaving the party, we saw red flashing police lights behind us and we got pulled over. This was about a month before my sixteenth birthday. I was busted for drinking from an open container and being underage. I got a ticket and there had to be a court appearance, so I had to tell my parents.

It was very shaming for them, and they were very bummed that I was in trouble with the law. I was embarrassed, too: in a small town like Jackson, everybody was obviously going to know that I had a court appearance. It also brought about an awareness that I would have to face ten years later in alcohol recovery, which was that I didn't get in trouble every time I drank, but every time I got in trouble I had been drinking.

I knew my parents were disappointed. They grounded me for two months, which turned out to be the only two months of continuous sobriety I would know for the next ten years. The upside is that because I came straight home after school each day I practiced bass a lot, which in some ways probably helped me to become a much better bassist, because I had no distractions. I made the appearance in court, where I got off lightly. The drinking laws weren't that strict at the time, so I got a slap on the wrist in the form of a small fine. The main thing was that I was still able to get my driver's license a month later. The bummer was that I was still grounded, so I couldn't go out and do anything with my friends. The truth is, I didn't use this time of reflection as a way to learn the lesson. Rather, I figured out how to avoid getting caught next time.

Looking back, I recall that sometimes my own life got a little dark, something I now know could have been a symptom of alcoholism later in my life. I distinctly remember going through three phases of fear as a kid. First, I had an extreme fear that the house was going to burn down: it was just a weird phase I went through. Then I thought I was going to be poisoned, because we were always out in the farm sheds where they had fertilizer and herbicides and oil, and I worried that I'd die if I ever accidentally licked my fingers. Then, when I was a teenager, I had an extreme fear of getting cancer. I don't know the significance of these phases, but they always seemed tied to some other insecurity. I know I was always afraid of my father's wrath, because he was a strict authoritarian. But as much as I feared my father, I thought like him in many ways. He was something of a single-minded, very focused, almost workaholic person. Being self-employed enabled him to be that way, another path I would follow in my adult years.

Farming can be a reclusive life, especially running farm machinery for days on end in the fields by yourself. My father wasn't the kind of guy who especially liked running the machinery: he seemed bored with it and became introspective. I was like that, too, for most of my life, starting with that little two-month grounding from my drinking escapades. Later I realized that this type of isolation thinking is a typical pattern of alcoholism, though I didn't know it at the time.

Through all this, my band Toz continued. Our drummer was a guy named Justin. He was an upbeat kind of guy. He liked rock 'n' roll, and he had girls around quite a bit. His sister Jane was actually my first girlfriend in the fourth grade, but she broke up with me, probably because I was too afraid to kiss her!

Jane and Justin's family was really cool and had a great energy about them. They lived on a lake in the Jackson area and let Toz play summer shows on their patio for all of their neighbors. Those were great summer days. Justin was always dating girls and in the high school social scene, and as a result I got plugged into that scene as well. Justin was the first musician I knew who actually got a real job as a dishwasher so he could have money to do things. In a way this was a drag, because we had to start planning our band rehearsals and gigs around his work schedule. Because my family had me doing farm work during the daytime, my evenings were free to rehearse and do shows. Not so with Justin, which was my first indicator that a job of any sort must never interfere with my music or band life.

Greg and I were now trying to write our own songs. We were the singers in Toz, though it was difficult for me because my voice was starting to change as I transitioned from childhood to manhood. Nonetheless, I was starting to move into professional show business, for all intents and purposes. I wore platform boots and scarves, trying to be as fashionable as a Jackson, Minnesota, rock star could be.

I was also the guy in the band who tended to the business of our bands. In this, of course, my father assisted me with the finances. He and I had many late-night conversations, with him philosophizing about life and the opportunities that lay ahead for me. With glass in hand, he would warn me of the dangers of the showbiz lifestyle, to which I was becoming accustomed. In many ways, the business attributes were the parts of my music lifestyle he could relate to, and that was his connection to my interest in the whole thing.

Meanwhile, I continued to be a reasonably good student. I enjoyed my English studies and even public speaking. I'm sure that led to my interests in writing, and explains why I'm not so shy in front of the camera or addressing large groups of people in a public forum. Different things come naturally to each of us, and those were natural to me. I also enjoyed history and social studies. The teachings in those courses seemed more applicable in my day-to-day life, and I've found them useful in my world travels, even to this day. I think I also found a connection with the teachers in those subjects, too, which always helped me excel in their classes.

I've looked back at my report cards, and it's obvious that when I applied myself and took an interest, I was pretty much a straight-B student, with the occasional A and C, depending on my interest in the subjects being taught. I could have been a straight-A student, but I can look at my reports now and see clearly which semester it was that I started smoking pot and drinking, because my grades suddenly became consistent C's and D's. When drugs and alcohol crept in, academics fell by the wayside.

Music was my savior in many ways, despite the associated habits. There was a kid on the school bus named Jason, a very rough, rebellious type of kid, who bullied me and called me "Little Gordy," because my dad's name was Gordon. He'd pick on me and smash my head against the window of the bus just for fun, and I never fought back because he would only have beaten me more. But when I was fifteen, and became known around town as the guy who played in rock bands, he started finding common ground with me and talking to me on the school bus about Ted Nugent. Suddenly there was no more banging my head against the window. By becoming a popular bassist in the area, I had gained his respect. That wouldn't be the last time the rebel crowd let me in because I was a musician. It taught me a survival skill, and one that appealed to my ego. If I was good at the bass, life would give me all that I needed. Including respect.

I was starting to lead a double life. I carried a secret around, especially in front of my dad, who was supporting my music career. His policy was "If you boys are going to drink, I'd rather you drank at home." This was a double-edged sword, because he really didn't want us drinking, but he knew we probably wouldn't drink because we were at home.

At the same time, my parents were throwing parties and drinking with their friends. I remember waking up one morning after my parents had a really big party, and they had a somber look on their faces.

They told me that a friend of theirs had drowned in our swimming pool the previous night while I was asleep. An ambulance had come and gone. That was a very sobering moment for everybody, and an indicator that as much fun as the party life could be, there were often serious consequences, too.

When I was sixteen we took a big family vacation, as we did every couple of years. We were taking a trip down to Florida, and we were going to stop at the Grand Ole Opry in Nashville to see some of the shows for a couple of nights. It was really painful for me, because Toz had a gig at a club called the Jackson Disco while I was away. The venue was owned by a local proprietor and was one of the only nightclubs in town. It was definitely a seedy scene, complete with alcohol and the associated nightlife. But it was a big thing for the band, and I had to turn it down to go on vacation with my family, which tore me apart.

Playing shows was becoming everything to me, and to have to cancel a show for any reason whatsoever was simply not acceptable in my book, even a dinky little gig like the one at the Jackson Disco. Performing in my band was my life. It was what I knew I was going to do forever. My parents said, "What, are you crazy? Family is everything!" but I was like, "Not when you're a rock 'n' roll musician!" In fact, I still struggle with this issue. Even though I'm a lot older and wiser these days and my kids mean the world to me, my passion for playing versus my commitment to family can be a real struggle—especially when you're wired for sound like I am.

I went into a music store in Atlanta when my family and I were on this vacation to Florida. At this point I had my Gibson EB-0 and Dan Armstrong basses, plus my Rickenbacker 4001, but I really wanted to get a B.C. Rich, because they were the cool metal axe at the time. They were very expensive, though. I remember seeing a Peavey T40 bass guitar, which was a good-sounding bass and fairly easy to play. It cost $240. But my dad asked, "Is that really the bass you want?" I said, "Well, really the bass I want is a B.C. Rich Mockingbird . . ." and he said, "How much is that?" I said, "Well, I know I can get one from this place called East Coast Sound in Danbury, Connecticut, for about nine hundred dollars." I was afraid to tell my dad this because I thought he'd freak out, but he came back with a statement that I've never forgotten.

He said, "You know, it's better to spend more money and buy right the first time, than to buy something you don't really want and have to keep going back and spending more money over and over again to get what you really wanted in the first place." He added, "If that's what you really want, why don't we set our sights on that, and I'll help you get it?" He came to me and found common ground there, and that was how we bonded on that vacation. I really started to appreciate his business acumen. Even though he didn't have a musical ear, he really did understand business, even as it applied to entertainment. There is a saying that goes "Give a man a fish, and you've fed him for a day. Teach a man to fish, and you've fed him for a lifetime." It turns out that sacrificing that gig back in Jackson for a family vacation gave me a chance to learn from my father a lesson about money that would feed me for a lifetime.

After the vacation we got that B.C. Rich Mockingbird bass, and it was the one I eventually took to California with me, the one that is in the earliest Megadeth photos from 1983 to '85.

Why did I want to go to California? Well, there were only a few places a budding rock star could really make it big: New York, London, or Los Angeles. L.A. seemed cool. It had sun, beaches, girls, and more recently big bands like Van Halen who were bringing a lot of attention to the music scene there. Plus, there was a group from the nearby town of Fairmont called Survivor, who were a really good band playing original music. They had played around the area back home, at places like the Jackson Disco, and at a nearby venue called the Fox Lake Ballroom, which was an old ballroom from the 1930s and '40s where people went in previous years to dance to swing bands. A lot of big groups out of Minneapolis would come and play at Fox Lake, and me, Greg, and my bandmates would always go to hear them play. We saw professional acts and watched how they were doing it.

In late 1979 or early 1980, the whole new-wave thing was coming around big-time, and the Cars were huge and the whole Gary Numan skinny-tie parade was on. This local band Survivor went to California and came back a year later with a new name—they'd really polished their act up, with skinny jeans and Capezio ballet shoes and really cool, fashionable short haircuts like Sting. It was totally impressive, and we were like, "Wow, these guys have been to rock school!" They'd sped all their tempos up, and their music was almost like a new-wave punk thing. That really made an impression on me.

That's why I thought I had to get out to California. Things were happening there. I'll never forget rehearsing on the farm in one of the barn buildings with my band, when I had the overwhelming feeling come over me that I had to get to L.A. as soon as possible. I immediately went up to the house and told my parents that I was going to dye my hair blond, put an earring in, change my name to David Schaller, and move to Hollywood that year. I still don't know why I chose the name Schaller, other than there were tuning pegs of that name. It sounded very rock 'n' roll. Plus, I didn't think Ellefson was a very show-biz name, so I needed something easier to pronounce.

My favorite new image was that of Rick Savage of Def Leppard, with the blond hair and the bass by the knees, the quintessential rock bassist. I was also watching Van Halen, who were just starting to pop at the time, and thought their look was so cool. Dean guitars had just come out, and they were supercool, too, along with B.C. Rich basses. I loved pointy guitars, and I wanted to move away from Fenders and Gibsons. I read magazine interviews with Eddie Van Halen, and I immersed myself into this new up-and-coming rock culture of the early 1980s.

Another reason I moved to California was that I didn't want to stay on the farm—it repelled me. I hated farm work because I hated being told what to do by my dad, who was very authoritarian. I also hated the physical labor. One chore that I especially hated was picking rocks out of the soil in the spring and summer. It is a common farm practice to drive across the fields and remove any large rocks that may damage the farm equipment during the next season of crop work. My buddies would come and help pick up those rocks, and my dad would yell at them—because for all intents and purposes, they were city kids and slackers who didn't have very strong work ethics.

One of the other brutal jobs was called "walking beans." On the farm you had rows of soybeans planted up and down the fields. In order to eliminate the weeds, we would employ up to thirty people to line up and walk down the rows to pull the weeds. It was hot, dirty, hateful work. I'd say "This is horrible. I certainly can't do this for the rest of my life!" and I couldn't wait to get back inside and plug in my bass and just lose myself in music and the continued thought of rock stardom. Music was my obsession; farm work was not.

That said, being raised on a farm kept me obedient, and there were times when I took pride in my farm work. A job well done does give you self-esteem. By my midteens I could drive a tractor. I learned to drive a car real young—long before I had a license—and I was responsible for it. I learned many wholesome skills that became helpful later in my life, and as I matured, I was actually proud that I learned them on a farm. But at the time, farm work ethics felt brutal.

I still managed to get into trouble. I skipped school one day and went over to Sioux Falls with my girlfriend, and we made up some story to tell our parents about staying at friends' houses so we wouldn't get caught. Sure enough, by the time we got home the next morning, our parents had put the story together. I was given the sex talk.

My dad said to me, "Sex is like shaving: once you start, you never stop. If you get some girl pregnant, the rest of your life is just gone, with all your dreams and aspirations." Again, he saw that I was really into music, having done it for a few years now and devoted every spare moment to it. He didn't want to see me blow it over getting a girl pregnant. Even more important, sex before marriage was against my church upbringing. To my father's credit, he started giving me safer farm work that meant there was no chance of losing a finger or getting hurt in machinery. He assigned me to jobs such as cleaning the pool and mowing the lawn, chores that needed to be done but that were quite safe from a career-threatening injury.

All these years later, when I look back at my childhood, it's not obvious why I later became addicted to drugs and alcohol. There was nothing in my background that made me predisposed to drink and take drugs. I wasn't abused and I was a reasonably happy kid with a secure background. But addiction is like Russian roulette. Some people can drink, take drugs, smoke pot, and even go further than that occasionally without much effect. Then they can stop doing those things without damage to their lives. However, for me there was a bullet in the chamber when I drank for the first time. This made it hard for me later on when I tried to face my addictions, because I thought, "I'm a pretty normal, well-adjusted guy: I'm not a screwup, except for when it comes to putting down drugs and alcohol. For some reason I just love to be high—not to escape anything—but just because I like to have a nice little buzz going on.

Even in my recovery, all these years later, I've met people whose backgrounds involved abuse, incest, jail terms, divorce, and so on, but I never experienced any of that, and it's made me wonder why I was an addict. I realized later that those things don't really have anything to do with addiction, although for some people they do form part of the road that leads to it. Ultimately the D-day is what happens the first time you put the substance into you, and that's what you have to deal with from that point onward.

Back to 1979. Right around this time, my buddies in Toz and I met a guitarist named Jerry Giefer, who came from Windom, Minnesota. He was a tall, lanky guy with long, black hair, and he could really shred on guitar. He was hands-down the most ripping guitarist any of us had heard locally, and he was our age! He could play beyond anything. More than that, he was really in touch with the New Wave of British Heavy Metal bands like Iron Maiden, Venom, Tank, and Motörhead. When we first met him, he walked in with Iron Maiden's first album and Motörhead's *No Sleep 'til Hammersmith*, and all of a sudden we lit up. Around this time our drummer, Justin, had just discovered the Scorpions' *Lovedrive* album, and we were like, "This is the next new thing!" This music didn't come from California; it was from Europe. Because it came from overseas, to us it had a certain magic about it. California was a long way away, but it was still attainable, whereas Europe felt like it wasn't.

I heard Iron Maiden and realized that Steve Harris was the bass player, the songwriter, and also the leader of the band, which really changed my assessment of a bass player's role in a band. I'd been listening to Geddy Lee of Rush a lot, and I was playing in the jazz band at school, too. I was taking bass lessons from our high school band instructor, Bob, who was an accomplished jazz head and a pretty good drummer. You could tell he had gigged out before he became a band teacher. He had long hair, and he would show up for jazz band rehearsal at 7 A.M. before school.

Thus began formal jazz studies for me and a friend, Ethan, with whom I carpooled from the farm on those mornings. Ethan was a great musician, and it was his mother who gave me my early Wurlitzer organ lessons during the fourth grade, which was my first official introduction to playing music. Jazz band actually made me feel better about jazz music in some way, as if it was rock 'n' roll of a different sort. Bob got me into Spyro Gyra and Weather Report, with their amazing bass player, Jaco Pastorius. I'd seen Stanley Clarke play on *The Midnight Special* at Greg's house years earlier, so I was already hip to some jazz bass playing.

Right about this time, the *Rocky* movie came out, and Maynard Ferguson, the trumpet player, wrote the theme song for it. One fall evening, Maynard played in the neighboring town of Windom, Minnesota, so Ethan and I went to see him. Even though I was into Rush and progressive music, I had never heard music played like this before. It seemed impossible to me to be this inhumanly good. Everybody in his band was unbelievably great. Weather Report drummer Peter Erskine was in his band, along with the Minneapolis bassist Gordon Johnson, who floored me with his fluid touch. As much as I respected Rush in the rock 'n' roll realm, they suddenly seemed like kindergarten musicians compared to Maynard's band.

In between playing in the school jazz band and listening to the other musicians I liked, I was exposed to a wide variety of music. I'd come home from school, put the needle on a record, and shred away on bass while listening to it. Toz was playing a lot of gigs. In order for our band to get hired, we had to do three or four sets a night, and we'd get maybe five hundred dollars. My dad bought us a trailer, and he also let us use the family van so we could have a vehicle to get to our shows. He even converted one of his sheds on the farm and put a furnace and insulation in it, so we could rehearse all year round.

Looking back on it, my father really stepped up to help us with all these band endeavors. He basically gave me a vehicle and a building, and he helped me buy a $5,000 PA system for the band. Those things helped me learn about mixing, EQ, crossovers, power amps, and how all those things in the signal path worked. In fact, I started experimenting with bi-amp and tri-amp bass rigs and even tore my PA apart to take components of it with me to L.A. a few years later. Some of that gear was actually used on Megadeth's first two studio albums.

Jerry joined our band, along with a new drummer named Brett Fredrickson, and started exposing us to the New Wave of British Heavy Metal. Because we had become so enamored with Iron Maiden's music, we changed the band name from Toz to Killers, as a tribute to Maiden's second LP. It's funny that in years to come, younger bands followed suit by naming themselves after Megadeth songs: the principle was exactly the same.

From playing with my bands, I'd learned that some songs move people on the dance floor and a lot don't. A lot of Killers' songs didn't. At the time a band out of Minneapolis called Chameleon, who had three or four records out, came into the area to perform. They were always on tour in the area, complete with their own original material, albums for sale, road crew, and semitruck. They were the real deal and their keyboard player was actually Yanni—yes, the Yanni who later became the famous New Age solo artist.

Killers actually opened up for Chameleon for a couple of shows, which was a major achievement, but showed me how far I still was from making it to the big time. This made me realize even more acutely that there was no way to make it big in Minnesota: I had to get to California.

I spent the next two years of my high school education filling out college entrance forms, but I didn't care about them because I knew I was going to California as soon as I graduated high school. I remember filling out a form once with my careers counselor, and it came back saying that due to my interests, I would be a really good forklift driver! I didn't care. I knew that what I wanted to do couldn't be measured by academic standards.

Around this time I had an interesting drug experience in high school. Somebody showed up at school with a bunch of Black Beauties, which are speed. I took a handful of them and got all fired up and excited. It happened to be the day when we were filling out our requests for classes for the next year, and I picked all these really difficult classes, going, "Trigonometry! Geometry! This will be great!"

At the beginning of the next school year, I got my schedule and I was like, "What in the world was I thinking when I filled this out? I can't take all these classes; I hate all this stuff!" I realized that it was because I'd been all jacked up on speed. So I immediately started dropping the classes so I could do study hall. That way, I could have an easy schedule and go back to the band room and practice bass in the soundproof practice cubicles every chance I could. I wasn't trying to be a dropout or a loser, but I wouldn't allow academics to get in the way of rock stardom. I made my life easy and got rid of the academics.

Killers split up by the fall of my senior year. I was now a guy without a band. This was when I started to realize that bands have personality problems and musical-direction shifts, and that splitting with your band is just like breaking up with a girlfriend: remaining friends afterward is near impossible. So I got interested in another band called Renegade, out of a little town called Estherville, Iowa, just over the border from Jackson. This band was a covers act with a few original songs. Like Killers, they were young guys from the same hometown but with a more mainstream set list, not so much a metal band. As a result, they did a lot of gigs and got paid well.

Renegade needed a bass player because their singer wanted to concentrate on vocals rather than playing bass, too. They had a really good guitarist who had just moved up from Cedar Rapids, Iowa, named Bill. He was a cool guy and I liked his style, so I auditioned. It was weird to audition, because I'd had my own band for so many years, but I played really well and got the gig—and next thing you know we're gigging, opening for Johnny Van Zant and other national bands, including Chameleon.

Renegade definitely took me to another level. The singer's dad, who was a high school teacher, was the manager. He was a bit like my dad; he looked after his son's band and made sure we didn't get ripped off. We were making money, and bought a school bus and converted it to a tour bus. Bill and I did a lot of drinking together; for a while he even lived at my house. We were always out late at night, drinking and hanging with girls.

In the fall of my senior year, we did a show, and someone at the show had some cocaine—from the Iowa cocaine cartel, mind you, which was not exactly Peruvian flake. So I snorted some up, but since I was sick with the flu, I didn't feel any effect. It felt rad, though, to be on a tour bus doing coke while playing in a band. In fact, I remember that the back of the April Wine album *Harder, Faster* had a band photo, and in it I swear the guitar player is holding a bag of coke in his hand just above the fingerboard. So here I was, living the dream, too.

Now I was seventeen, nearly eighteen, and there was a part of me that was going, "Okay, I get this. Now I'm an adult." Over the next couple of months, Bill and I dropped out of Renegade. We didn't want to be there anymore, which was an interesting lesson for me. I realized that I am not a guy who can just take a gig only to make money, and I can't take a gig just to be playing: there has to be a means to an end with it. The music has to be intrinsically intertwined into my DNA. Renegade's music wasn't metal: it was more like Loverboy than Iron Maiden, and my heart was definitely not into it. Plus, I knew I needed to get to California, so my days in the Midwest were numbered.

I was completely steeped in Maiden at the time. I went up to Minneapolis to see them play with the Scorpions and Girlschool. It must have been 1982, and I knew that was what I wanted to do. It was definitely my future to play the newer style of metal music. Maiden brought metal home to me. It wasn't wimpy and glittery; it was cool and accessible. What they did in the New Wave of British Heavy Metal was very similar, in that sense, to what Megadeth later did in thrash metal, in that it was music inspired by a real street-level honesty.

I completed my classes and graduated high school in late May 1983. That month I'd started investigating the Bass Institute of Technology in Hollywood, California, which was really coming of age. A lot of cool guys were teaching there, like bassists Tim Bogert and Jeff Berlin, and it was a hip one-year school for guys like me who wanted a foray into the L.A. music scene. It provided education and, hopefully, the skills required to survive the scene in Los Angeles. I thought this was my ticket to L.A., because I could tell my parents I was going to school there—and what parent doesn't want their kid to go to school? It was a one-year vocational music course in Hollywood, so it was a fraction of the cost of a four-year degree at a university. I applied and got accepted.

So that was it. Greg and I, plus two friends, Brad Schmidt and Brent Giese from the neighboring town of Windom, Minnesota, moved to Hollywood together five days after graduating high school at the end of May in 1983. We got into my van, hooked up a U-Haul trailer, and drove off. My parents waved us good-bye. I remember so clearly driving down the driveway of my house on the farm, turning left to go south, and looking back—and there they were, waving. No doubt my mother was crying as her little boy headed west to pursue his dream in the big city of Hollywood. I'll have that vision for the rest of my life.

Driving to Los Angeles took four days, and we partied all the way to California. Game on.

A THOUGHT

Follow Your Instincts

A defining moment on my musical journey happened at the age of sixteen on the farm in Minnesota. My band was rehearsing in one of my dad's work sheds, and out of nowhere the thought hit me that I had to get out to Los Angeles as soon as possible. It was such a powerful conviction that it suddenly precluded everything else in my life. That became the driving force for the remainder of my high school years, and ultimately led me out the door to L.A. upon graduation.

The events that took place from there can only be described as divine inspiration and guidance. So often, that little voice inside, often in the form of gut instinct, is the one that needs to be obeyed in order for us to know the path we're meant to follow.

CHAPTER THREE

California Dreaming

"Discipline, not desire, determines the outcome of our lives."
—Dr. Charles Stanley

Man, I hated Los Angeles. I'd seen the city on TV, and it had looked beautiful; but when I got there, I thought it was the pits. There was a ton of traffic and way too many people. To come from a rural farm in Minnesota to Hollywood couldn't have been a bigger 180-degree shift for me. I was bummed, but I couldn't go home unless I wanted to suck it up and be a farmer, which I wasn't prepared to do. I'd never thought of any other career besides music and rock stardom.

The only connection that any of us had in Los Angeles was a woman named Alvira, from a neighboring town in Minnesota. The Bass Institute of Technology's apartment referral system had passed us on to her. Alvira was from Mountain Lake, a town about a half hour from Jackson, so there was a nice little connection there. In hindsight, I'd like to think that God somehow lined all that up. She had an apartment building that she managed with her husband at 1736 North Sycamore in Hollywood, at the intersection of Hollywood Boulevard and

Sycamore, right by La Brea and two blocks from Mann's Chinese Theatre. That was where Greg, Brad, Brent, and I moved to straight from the cornfields of rural Minnesota. Greg and I had one apartment and the other guys had the one next door.

We moved into our apartment around June 1, 1983. We wanted to start meeting some people, and one day Brad said, "I saw this guy walking around. He had long blond hair and he was barefoot, and he looked like a rock 'n' roll guy!" We decided to try and meet this dude: maybe he could become a buddy.

A couple of days later, Greg and I woke up in our little studio apartment and started jamming some tunes. I was playing the introduction to "Running with the Devil" by Van Halen at about nine or ten o'clock in the morning, when all of a sudden we heard this loud "Shut up!"

Something came crashing down on our window air conditioner. We looked out and saw a ceramic flowerpot. We stopped playing. My first thought was, "People in Hollywood aren't very friendly, are they?" Where we grew up on the farm, we left our keys in the car and our houses unlocked, and people would drop by whenever they wanted. Everybody knew each other, and it was very "come as you are." Now I'm in Hollywood—and this is my first introduction to my neighbors.

Within a day or so, Brad confirmed that the blond-haired, barefoot guy he had seen was the dude who lived upstairs from us. So one night, a day or two later, we went upstairs and knocked on the door. We heard some music playing through the door and thought, "That's got to be him."

Dave Mustaine cracked the door open, with the chain still on it, looked out and gave us the infamous Mustaine smirk. He had a glass of wine or cognac in his hand and said, "Who is it?"

I said, "Hey, er, we live downstairs. Do you know where we can buy some cigarettes?" He gave us a snarl and said, "Down the street on the corner," and slammed the door in our faces.

We stood there and Greg said, "That was definitely the guy—but that didn't go very well. Let's try a new approach." So we knocked again.

He cracked open the door again. "What?" Mustaine asked, clearly annoyed.

We were like, "Hey, do you know where to get any beer?"

He paused for a minute. Then, realizing that although we looked like hoodlums, we were pretty harmless guys who just wanted to hang out, he finally unlatched the chain and said, "All right, come on in."

Though at first Dave appeared skeptical, he made us feel at home. There was a singer there named Lor, a big, tall, black-haired, sunglasses-wearing, Nikki Sixx look-alike—a guy Dave was working with on some new songs. He was dark and menacing in appearance, but he was actually a friendly guy. Dave's roommate, Tracy, was there, too. Music was playing, and it wound up being a very casual, sociable evening.

We decided to go down to the corner liquor store, right on the corner of Hollywood Boulevard and Sycamore, where Dave—who was the California legal drinking age of twenty-one, while the rest of us were eighteen—picked up a case of Heineken for all of us. I noticed as we walked back to the apartment that with his flip-flops and blond hair, Dave had this typical California surfer look. He had the case of beer up on his shoulder as he was walking, and he told us stories about some band he'd been in called Metallica, which none of us had ever heard of, but he was a good storyteller, and we were wide-eyed with wonder.

Although his tone was angry and resentful when he mentioned Metallica, you could tell he was proud of his achievements with them and that he had been around the block a time or two in show business. I was intimidated but impressed. Having had my own experiences over the last several years gigging in the Midwest bar and ballroom circuits, I was intrigued to learn how the scene operated on the bigger stages, where I soon learned that Dave was a budding celebrity rock star.

In the apartment Dave had two Marshall half-stacks and a B.C.

Rich Bich guitar, which he'd brought back on the bus from New York after his stint with Metallica a couple of months before. He played a couple of songs for us. They included an untitled song, which would go on to be "Devil's Island" on the *Peace Sells... but Who's Buying?* album, and essentially his first post-Metallica song, "Megadeath." That song was later retitled "Set the World Afire" but it didn't get released until the *So Far, So Good... So What!* record in 1988. It had been inspired on his bus ride home from New York, when he'd seen a quote on a handbill from California senator Alan Cranston, who said, "The arsenals of megadeath can't be rid," meaning that America had built up so much nuclear firepower that we couldn't get rid of it, no matter what we did. That was the basis of the song.

I remember hearing those songs and going, "Wow!" It was really heavy, unique music, and scary-sounding because it was so dark. Immediately, there was something extremely compelling about Dave and his music. While he carried himself with the air of my teenage idol David Lee Roth from Van Halen, he had modern-day skills that went a step beyond the New Wave of British Heavy Metal that had inspired me just a few years prior. Clearly, he was the real deal.

The next day, Greg was really enthused. He was like, "We gotta play with that guy! We should go back up there and hook up with him." But I was thinking, "Man, I'm way out of my depth here." I knew I was a good bass player, but playing with this guy would mean taking a huge leap in my life, which was not simply about playing the notes on a bass. I'd be taking a step up to a whole new level, in terms of my lifestyle as well as musically.

But Greg pushed back. He was a loudmouth with an attitude: rebellious toward his parents, and he'd always been in trouble in school. Simply put, he was the perfect fit for rock 'n' roll. I, on the other hand, was more mild-mannered because I'd been raised in a very different home. Without Greg, I don't know that I would have had the fortitude to go up and knock on Dave's door.

BIT wasn't scheduled to start for about eight weeks, which allowed me some time to find my way around L.A., find part-time employment, and give my life some stability. But this move to hook up with Dave was like starting a crash course in showbiz only a week after high school, and it instantly changed the direction of my life, possibly forever. I wanted in, but I knew it would be immediate and that there would be no summer vacation. This would be the beginning of the rest of my life. As scared as I was, I knew I had to do it.

As for Dave, he was sizing us up. He is a quick study in people's character, and as much as we thought we were ultra-cool hoodlums, I think he quickly knew we were pretty harmless young lads doing our best to dress the part of rural metalheads.

But there was no going back. A couple of days later, we were hanging with Dave and playing some songs together. Dave had another guy there named Matt Kisselstein, a kid from Beverly Hills who was playing bass. Matt had been a bassist for about a year and I liked him, but he eventually conceded that it made sense for me to be the bass player. In fact, when we went through Dallas on the *Risk* album tour in 1999, at a radio station we visited, Matt was in upper management. He got to do what he was good at, and so did I. We had a good laugh about how things turned out.

Right from the beginning, Dave was earnestly formulating ideas for a new band, his first post-Metallica venture. This wasn't just some random jamming hangout situation. Dave was creating something totally new, and he was determined to call the shots and be in charge. In most of my bands in Minnesota, I had been largely in charge; but this move now required that I be subordinate to Dave, which was not easy, due to my take-charge attitude. But this was not music that you could hear at the time from any other band. I had been mostly playing bass with my fingers, even though I had been a pick player as well. I'd honed my chops on Steve Harris's playing in early Iron Maiden and Bob Daisley in Rainbow and Ozzy Osbourne's band—both of whom were different stylistically from what Dave's music required. Despite the learning curve, Dave said, "You're definitely a good bass player. You've got chops, and you know what you're doing"—which translated to "I can work with you."

Another incentive for bringing me into the band was that I had a van, so now Dave had transportation. I don't fault him for it, and to his credit, he was resourceful, a skill I quickly learned from him in order to survive in big-city show business. Dave's persona cast a big shadow over me. Because the band was his vision, and we were together as a team in the early days, I was pretty much at the beck and call of the band and my duties to it, which was sometimes tough on my self-esteem. Often I wished for my own life, so I could grow up a bit on my own; but as long as we were forging the cast for the group, that wasn't going to happen. My life was simply not going to be my own at this point in the game.

I smoked lots of pot and drove around L.A. with Dave directing the way, which is how I learned the streets and freeways of the area, completely stoned out of my mind. I went wherever Dave needed me to go. It was a mutually beneficial relationship: I had something he needed, and he was the equivalent of a big brother and mentor to me—someone who could show me the ropes and someone with a clear vision of what he wanted to achieve with his band and music. We moved forward together.

We jammed through the month of June. After a couple of weeks, Dave had Lor as the singer, me as the bassist, and Greg as the other guitar player: the beginnings of a real group. Dave's original working title of the band was Fallen Angel, although you could tell he wasn't sold on it. One day, after we'd been rehearsing over by Forest Lawn Mortuary in Burbank, we were in our downstairs apartment trying to think of a band name. Either Greg or Lor said, "Why don't we call ourselves Megadeath?" That's what turned the corner, and because Dave had some experience with numerology he figured out that by dropping the *a* in *Megadeath*, you'd have eight letters, which was the perfect number, because 8 is the symbol of infinity, rotated 90 degrees. Every single thing in our band was very much thought out, very methodical.

No details were left to chance, from the guitars we played to the shoes, stretch jeans, and leather jackets we wore.

Even our names were carefully thought out. Right from the beginning Dave said, "We can't have two Daves in the band. What's your middle name?"

"Warren," I said.

"Maybe we should call you War?" Lor suggested, but I didn't think that was cool and neither did Dave. I agreed that we needed to do something about this name thing, though. We were friends with a guy named Peyton, who shared an apartment with his sister and her husband just south of Santa Monica Boulevard. He had been to BIT and was a driven and creative sort of character who was also a fantastic paint artist. One day we were at the grocery store on Santa Monica Boulevard, and Peyton said something about how I'd just come from the farm or just arrived on the turnip truck, and therefore I was "Junior Dave," as if I was just a naïve farm boy.

Dave started cracking up. "Junior! That's great. Junior!" And the name stuck. I hated it. I felt it was completely condescending, and even though I accepted it as my new moniker, it bothered me for the next twenty years. I didn't like being labeled a wet-behind-the-ears farm boy. I don't look at it the same way now, but it irritated me at the time.

I knew my place was with Dave. I certainly didn't consider going home an option. What was I going to do—help my brother on the farm? I never had a backup plan, but I look on that as a blessing. I had a calling to go forward and do this music thing. I knew I had to do it. Ironically, as much as I had family and other financial resources upon which I could have drawn, I never did. I never moved back home, I never called home for money: I figured if I was there to stake my claim, then I had to suck it up and make it work. Years later my mother disclosed to me that she and my dad realized that they had never had to put me through college, so giving me the family van and a credit card with a five-hundred-dollar limit, which I always paid off myself, was a pretty light load for launching their son into the adult world.

When we met Dave, Greg and I needed jobs to make some money. I had brought seven hundred dollars of savings with me to California, and I had the credit card my dad had given me, but little else. Dave had a job in phone sales at an office down in Culver City, setting up appointments for solar energy companies to sell solar panels. Dave helped me, Greg, Brad, and Brent all get jobs there to get on our feet with our relocation. It was a staggered, commission-based gig—if we set up an appointment, we'd get twenty-five dollars, and if that led to a sale there'd be another fifty dollars in the back end—and probably a scam job. Since we could all talk on the phone, we were each pointed to a cubicle and told to pick up the phone and start "smiling and dialing." Our new employment worked out well for Dave, too, because now he had an easy way to get to work—in my van.

During my interview, the guy who ran the company said to me, "Look, man, if you're gonna be in the music business you're gonna be selling yourself, and that's why this phone sales thing is good for you. It's a great way for you to learn how to sell yourself. I realize you're not going to do this forever, but it's a chance for you to come out of your shell." I hated this, perhaps because I knew it was true. I also hated trying to make people buy something they didn't want. I wasn't an extrovert, unlike so many people I saw in L.A. But Dave was really good at it. With his California street smarts, his storytelling, and his gift for gab, he could go from having two appointments on the wall to fifteen or eighteen by the end of the day. He was definitely a survivor. In any situation, he could turn on the charm to provide for himself.

After that, we took jobs in another phone sales place, run by an aggressive little guy whom we really looked up to because he was a kind of father figure. We worked a few of these phone sales jobs, but by August, Brad and Brent had turned around and headed back home to Minnesota. They were like, "This is not for us: we're not meant to be here."

After a while, Dave and I realized that Greg wasn't working out in the band either. Although he was a nice guy and could play reasonably well, he didn't look the part and was too laid back to to be a productive member of a group. What he was really after was a summer vacation. We'd party and have fun together, but the band was the band, and we were focused on world domination. So one day we went down to the apartment and Dave delivered the news to him. It was hard. I don't think I said much at all, other than that I'd go and get my stuff together because I was moving out of the apartment we shared on Sycamore.

Greg Handevidt (school friend):

David and Mustaine came down to the apartment. I remember Mustaine telling me that I was out, and David just looked down at his feet. I was angry and resentful. The funny thing was that a couple of weeks later Mustaine came over and asked me to come back. I did a couple more rehearsals with them, but it didn't feel right. Anyway, I don't hold grudges—I'm not that kind of person—and my resentment didn't last. I wasn't going to let something like that destroy my friendship with David, whom I'd known since I was a little kid. It would have been really petty to do that.

It was sad, but it needed to happen. He went back to Minnesota and played in a band called Kublai Khan before joining the navy and living in San Diego. He's a lawyer now and one of my best friends.

After that, we moved out of our apartment and in with Peyton, his sister, and her husband—although they weren't exactly thrilled about it. Dave and I developed a habit of just moving in with people, and then we'd use their phone and split the groceries. We didn't want to squat, but we had to—it was musician survival stuff. We were essentially homeless for about two years as we got the band off the ground. We hated it, but we did what we had to do.

Now I was the only remaining Minnesota guy out there in California, out of the four of us who'd headed west, which definitely took me out of my comfort zone. This gave me the liberty to decide that if we were going to make this band happen, I needed to pay attention. Making Megadeth work professionally was a job: you showed up on time, you put on a uniform, and you obeyed the rules, as any good employee should.

Even at that young age, I was starting to get my Megadeth act together on every level: how I talked, how I played, even what I thought. That year, 1983, was a serious wake-up call in my life. I had to jump into the shark tank and learn to swim with the best of these guys—or be eaten myself. It was that simple.

Dave recognized that he had street smarts and I didn't, and while I think in his heart he wanted to be friends before bandmates, his street-smart drive told him that the band's success had to be the priority. In the early days, I could see that people were really attracted to Dave and genuinely interested in the status of his developing band. I remember going down to the Troubadour with Dave one night, where W.A.S.P. was playing with a band called Hellion, who were coming up the ranks and had a female singer named Ann Boleyn. Dave introduced me as Junior, his new bass player, which led to an onslaught of questions about whether or not I was as good as Cliff Burton, Metallica's bassist.

Cliff was a very innovative player in metal, and Dave knew I'd be compared to him, so he had high standards for me. I had to be more than just good, I had to be great. Fortunately, having had some formal jazz studies, I understood and appreciated Cliff's skills. Specifically, I think what endeared metal fans to Cliff was his use of arpeggios and a distorted wah pedal: it was a cool combination of shred meets virtuoso.

My approach, however, came more equally from a rock and jazz perspective, influenced by bassists such as Jaco Pastorius and Stanley Clarke. To my mind, what those guys were doing was inhuman—stuff from another planet altogether. Regardless, as bassists like Cliff and me started to incorporate other styles and genres into our bass playing, the metal fans loved it. This enthusiastic response to my playing from the fans fueled my and Dave's drive to really put the bass out front in our songs. To some degree, I think Dave didn't just see me as worthy of being compared to Cliff; he saw me as a secret weapon that he could deploy to show the world that his new band could live up to, and even be better than, anything Metallica could do, even with regard to innovative bass playing.

Ultimately, I had to take everything I'd ever learned from playing in a jazz band, learning Iron Maiden licks, and playing in a cover band—all the things I'd done back in Minnesota—in order to partner up with Dave and create something different. This was no time to be a lone wolf. Shortly thereafter, we recruited a new drummer, Lee Rausch.

Just prior to this, Megadeth had another drummer in 1983 named Dijon Carruthers, who was really into Ritchie Blackmore and Deep Purple. His dad was an actor named Ben Carruthers, who had been in films like *The Dirty Dozen*. Dijon was a solid double-bass drummer, heavily into British drum god Cozy Powell. He had a twisted sense of humor but did not do any drugs. His offbeat sensibilities helped him pen the original lyric to the song "Black Friday," which appeared on the *Peace Sells . . .* album. At one point Dijon tried to convince me to move to England with him, which I thought was bizarre. Still, we got on well together, although he didn't stay in Megadeth for long.

I remember Dave and I went over to Dijon's apartment in the Fairfax and Santa Monica area of Hollywood on my nineteenth birthday in November 1983, and I attempted to drink nineteen shots of tequila. I think I got as far as thirteen. I was hungover for two days, and that was the last time I ever drank that stuff.

Dave was writing songs all the way through 1983, and after some early rehearsals at a little room off Sunset Boulevard, right opposite the Chateau Marmont, we had the beginnings of "Looking Down the Cross," "Devil's Island," and "Set the World Afire." Dave was also working on "The Skull Beneath the Skin," which had the original working title of "Self Destruct." The tempos were slow, with a cool, groovy feel. They had a heavy, Black Sabbath kind of vibe, which caught the attention of everyone who heard them.

We auditioned all these Sunset Boulevard kinds of singers before Dave became the singer of Megadeth. It happened on New Year's Eve when we were rehearsing close to downtown L.A. at an old brewery converted to a rehearsal hall, run by a hustling local musician type known as Curly Joe. We rented space from him to rehearse in his facility, and on this night yet another singer flaked out on his audition with us. At the time, Dave wrote all the lyrics, so now it seemed he should sing his own songs. I remember the first time he did it: he was all red-faced afterward because he didn't know how to breathe properly and sing, but it was obviously going to work.

I remember being very encouraging to him about this. Dave never viewed himself as a singer, but he is an artist in every sense of the word, and sometimes the quality of a singer's voice is second to the conviction of their words, especially in metal music. That was a huge lesson for me as I was sowing my own oats as an artist. Perfection is not always needed, but conviction is, and Dave had that quality to his singing.

We played a few shows with Kerry King of Slayer on guitar in early 1984. He had a B.C. Rich guitar, which we liked because it meant he was thinking like us. We'd considered a few different guitarists, including Jim Durkin from Dark Angel, but Kerry was the only one who came in and nailed the music right away. I remember that Dave showed him some riffs—really complex stuff—and Kerry instantly mirrored it and played it right back at him, note for note. I was flabbergasted. It was like he was part of Dave's DNA. To this day, Kerry is still one of the best rhythm guitar players that was ever in Megadeth.

Kerry King (Slayer): I met David for the first time a couple of weeks before I played five shows with Megadeth, back in February 1984. I was stoked to do it: I joined them because I'd seen Mustaine play with Metallica, and I was genuinely impressed. I thought the guy could play, and when I heard he was looking for a guitar player, I thought I'd try out because in my eyes he was awesome. Ellefson was a really good bassist. He's always been a cool guy, and he's always been genuine. I really liked Megadeth's early stuff.

After those first Megadeth shows in the Bay Area in February and April 1984, I could see that the fire to rekindle Slayer was truly alive in Kerry's eyes. It was as if the Bay Area shows with us opened his eyes to another way of doing it, different from how it was done in L.A. with hairdos, makeup, studded belts, and so on. I truly believe that those early shows with Kerry set a new course for him to reinvigorate Slayer and allowed them to be the global phenomenon they are today.

So Kerry returned to Slayer, and once again it was just me and

Dave. However, by May 1984, we had started to get label and management interest, especially from Brian Slagel at Metal Blade and Walter O'Brien at Combat Records, who would later manage Pantera. In the middle of 1984, we were put in touch with a guy named Jay Jones, who became a kind of quasi-manager to Megadeth. He introduced us to a drummer, Gar Samuelson, because our first drummer, Lee Rausch, had told us he needed to go up into the mountains and find himself—and that was the last we ever heard of him.

In mid-1984 Gar joined the band. He was a very avant-garde drummer: he did a progressive jazz thing and cited Billy Cobham and Keith Moon as his two main influences. Initially I wasn't particularly keen on his style—which was a light, wispy kind of fusion drumming—because I'd been visualizing the drum style of Clive Burr of Iron Maiden or Phil Taylor from Motörhead. Gar was formerly in another band called the New Yorkers with a guitarist named Chris Poland. Jay Jones wanted Chris to audition for us because he had fancied himself as a quasi-manager of the New Yorkers a few years prior.

Chris Poland (ex-Megadeth): The first time I met David was at the Waters Club in San Pedro. Megadeth was a three-piece band, and Gar had asked me to come down to see them, because he wanted me to be the second guitarist. I rented a room at Mars Studios, where the two Daves both worked, and I took all my gear down there and played for a couple of hours. Then Dave Mustaine knocked on the door and asked, "You're Chris, right? Do you want to join the band?" and I said, "Yes!"

Chris was really good, but now we had a situation where Dave and I were the two metal guys and Gar and Chris were the jazz guys. Initially it wasn't always a good fit. Chris was the first real jazz musician drug addict I had met.

My father always told me, "Whatever you do, don't take cocaine," so I said, "Of course not, Dad, I would never do that." But in the back of my mind I was thinking, "Man, I can't wait to get out there and do some of that coke," because it just seemed like the L.A., rock 'n' roll thing to do.

My relocation to L.A. allowed me to re-create myself in whatever way I wanted. That's dangerous when you're only eighteen, and you don't know exactly who you want to be. I hadn't been to college, and all of a sudden I was leaping out of the nest for the first time: from the humble, wholesome farm in Minnesota to what is probably one of the most decadent, seedy places on the planet—the armpit of Hollywood.

As we put the various lineups of Megadeth together and as drug use increased, every lineup became darker and more corrupt and sinister. It started with pot and beer when Dave and I first met, and then guys started coming around with cocaine—and then in 1984 I discovered a new drug, one that would have devastating consequences.

A THOUGHT

On the Road

My move to California was not an easy road to hoe. A lesson I quickly learned is that opportunity is often disguised as hard work. My early days in L.A. were downright painful and horrifying at times, but being young, I was resilient and able to bounce back quickly. I also know now that if you're going to go after a seemingly impossible dream, you'd better try it while you're young, especially in the music business. My theory became that eighteen years of age might be too young, but by twenty-one you might be too old.

While age may not be a factor in many lines of work, showbiz likes the young. I believe this is largely because of looks and agility, but also because young people are idealists and willing to put everything on the line, while naïvely allowing themselves to be manipulated. However, if a threat to your dream is on the line, it's easy to be motivated. You'll do things you never thought you were capable of doing in order to see your dreams come true.

The upside is that as a youngster, you also have time to recover from setbacks. So often, our youthful energy and ideals give us the strength to overcome the obstacles in our path to success.

CHAPTER FOUR

Back to the Womb

"If you hang out in a barbershop long enough, you're eventually going to get a haircut."

—Anonymous

I remember clearly the first time I took heroin.

Dave and I were rehearsing with Gar and Chris, whose jazz background had given them a kind of smoky, barroom mind-set when it came to heroin. Gar warned me not to try it, but I was curious and asked him what it felt like. He said, "Dude, it's like going back to your mother's womb: it's like swimming in a bowl of liver." I also remember him telling me, half-jokingly, "Hey dude, if you really wanna be great, try some of this. If you wanna be great, you gotta do heroin!" He even made a joke along the lines of "Think about all the people that did it, like Charlie Parker and Jimi Hendrix." I was thinking of Janis Joplin and Sid Vicious, who both died of overdoses. Eventually my curiosity won out, and I decided to try some.

I discovered that snorting heroin brought me down off cocaine. Soon I was doing heroin as often as I was also doing coke. It was like that with a lot of things: the first time I drank I thought, "This isn't

Chris Poland (ex-Megadeth): David was sober up to the point when there was no way he could be sober anymore, because there was too much bad stuff going on that he got involved with. He wasn't a bad person, but he got dragged into bad situations.

bad—it's awesome!" Then a couple of months later I tried pot and I was like, "This is awesome, too!" Then I did some cocaine and I thought, "Okay, this feels kinda funny—but I'm not dead, and I'm not in jail, so it can't be that bad." They teach you in high school that every drug is a gateway to the next drug, and they're right, because the next thing I knew, there I was on heroin.

I remember very clearly in 1984 when Combat Records put Megadeth under contract. We got an $8,000 advance and went into the studio in December of that year to record our first album, *Killing Is My Business . . . and Business Is Good!* It was around this time that I finally realized that I had a problem with heroin. I'd been partying a lot, and doing smack and coke for a few days in a row, on and off for several months. Then one day I didn't do any—and I woke up feeling really crummy. I snorted up some heroin, and all of a sudden I felt great. That's when I thought, "Uh-oh . . . I think I understand why our guitarist and drummer have to score before they rehearse." It was about "getting well," as we called it; or "getting the monkey off my back." I'd stepped over a line I never thought I would cross. I was becoming a bona fide addict after only a single year in Los Angeles. By mid-1984 I was drinking, smoking pot, using cocaine, and taking heroin. Those became my Four Horsemen of the Apocalypse.

I was never a huge fan of psychedelic drugs. I took acid once and didn't really enjoy the effects. The next day I was in a very deep, reflective frame of mind: sometimes I wonder to this day if that one trip changed me permanently. I became a much more thoughtful, cautious character afterward, and not in a good way. My one experience with mushrooms was absolutely horrifying. Never again.

I could feel the drugs interfering with my vision for my life and my passion for rock 'n' roll. Other people could handle it. I felt as if I'd sold my soul.

Meanwhile, we made the first Megadeth album. Eight thousand dollars wasn't a lot to make a record with, even back then, and we probably spent half of it on lifestyle and living expenses. We moved in with our coproducer Karat Faye, who had once been a staff engineer at the famed Record Plant. He had big stories about the rock stars he'd met in the business over the years, which impressed me.

Scott Ian (Anthrax): I think I first met David in the summer of 1984, when Anthrax played in Los Angeles for the first time, at the Country Club in Reseda. I have pictures of us backstage, where Dave Mustaine played me recordings of the *Killing Is My Business . . .* tracks. Whenever I've met Ellefson, he's always been the nicest guy. He's a sweetheart and a great bass player. The fact that he was playing with a pick, when most bassists in the genre were using their fingers, and [that] he didn't simply follow the guitar part like most bass players was really amazing. He really kept it musical.

We went up to Indigo Ranch Studio in Malibu to do the album and stayed at the guesthouse there, the bummer being that there was just one very narrow dirt road leading to it, and whenever we ran out of drugs we had to either drive back down the hill or call one of our Hollywood friends to bring some drugs up to us, which was a nuisance. I remember one night, when I was very high on cocaine, *Scarface* was on TV. It scared the living daylights out of me. That's not a good film to see if you're high on coke! I saw my future in that film and it looked pretty freaky.

I was intensely aware of what I was doing to myself, even if I wasn't honest about it with anyone else. In recovery we talk about rigorous honesty being required in order to get sober and stay that way, and I'd been honest with myself all along—just not with other people. I would call my parents and tell them what was going on with the band, without ever telling them about any drug use. I acted as if I was keeping it all together, even though I was essentially homeless and squatting in people's houses.

Chris Poland (ex-Megadeth): Ellefson would say, "I know a guy on the other side of town who has some tar, let's go over there." We would buy eighty dollars' worth of heroin and do it right there. I think that was the first time he realized just how bad things had become. Once you're there, it's hard to walk away from it. It was tough. It never should have happened. A lot of that pain and anger came out in Megadeth's music: the drugs really fueled the fire in the band.

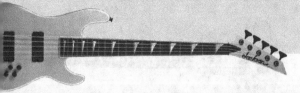

We made *Killing Is My Business . . .* in December 1984. All of us were strung out to some degree during the sessions—Chris completely so; Gar a little less because he had to keep it together for his job as a general manager at B.C. Rich Guitars. I was the fun, happy partier who was getting in way too deep.

Making the album was pretty exhilarating, although the sound quality wasn't great, because we had so little money for it. I liked *Killing Is My Business . . .*, but I wish some of the tempos had been a bit less extreme. We'd originally rehearsed the songs significantly slower, but Megadeth's music had suddenly gotten much faster back in the fall of 1983 when Dave received a letter from a fan, forwarded to him by our friend Brian Lew, who was helping us out, acting as a fan-club go-between. Metallica had just released their debut album, *Kill 'Em All*, and this fan had written, "Dave, I hope your songs are faster than Metallica's." The next day we sped up all the songs by about forty beats per minute. Extreme speed was deemed the cool factor in thrash metal back in those days, and that one fan letter changed Megadeth's sound overnight.

Our version of Nancy Sinatra's "These Boots Are Made for Walkin'" was a comedy cover, for sure, but I think Jay Jones—whose idea it was—saw the storyteller, raconteur side of Dave and knew that he could do a real tongue-in-cheek version of it. It worked well and lightened the mood of the album a little bit.

We turned in the record to Combat in January 1985. By then Chris was pretty much out of the band. His addiction had really taken over, and made it impossible for him to remain with Megadeth.

In the spring of 1985, we were still short a guitarist. We were supposed to hit the road, and our backs were against the wall. Jay Jones introduced us to Mike Albert, a seasoned musician who had played guitar with Captain Beefheart. He became the fill-in guitar player for the Killing Is My Business . . . tour: five or six weeks across the U.S. as the support act to the Canadian band Exciter, who also had a new album out.

Mike Albert was a seasoned touring musician. He was concerned about the tour income, which we knew was going to be very low from the start. He was in his early thirties, a decade older than Dave and me.

I was the only guy in the band with a credit card, despite being the youngest member, and believe me, we used every nickel it afforded us. Dave was an optimist, though, and he could see the big picture. Plus, we had no other options anyway. I knew what I wanted to do with my life and I felt sure what my destiny was, so we went for it.

The tour commenced in June 1985 in Baltimore. I remember Gar flew in late from New Orleans, where he was exhibiting with B.C. Rich Guitars at the National Association of Music Merchants (NAMM) show, his day job at the time. Because of this, Exciter had to go on first, which was a great way to start the tour.

On the way to the third show, in Cleveland, our van broke down, leaving us by the side of the freeway. Our New York tour manager Frank Pappitto and I hitched a ride for a couple of exits and suddenly saw a National car rental outlet, right there under a streetlight, at eleven o'clock at night. It was surreal. We went in, rented a Chevy Caprice on my credit card, went back to pick up the other guys, and transferred all our stuff from the van into the car. It was a brutal night drive, with all of us squished together.

Early the next morning, Gar was driving, and at one point he turned around to help me move one of his kick drum pedals, which was crammed behind his seat. As he was doing this, he took his eyes off the road just long enough to lose control of the car, and we went flying off the road at eighty miles per hour. We hit a road sign, which sheared off and flew over us as we careened into a ditch on the side of the road. I thought we were dead; I truly thought that this was the end. It was one of the most frightening experiences of my life.

The car hit the ditch and came to a screeching halt. We were all freaking out. A boom box sitting in the back window above me had hit me on the back of my neck, which really hurt. I got out of the car and saw a semitruck, which had stopped to see what had happened. The driver got out and asked if we were okay. I answered, "Yeah, I think there was a deer in the road!" He rolled his eyes with a kind of amused skepticism and helped us pull the car out of the ditch. We had to put the spare tire on the car to carry on. So there we were, driving along with a replacement tire and weeds sticking out of the side of the car, looking like the Beverly Hillbillies, rolling in to gig number three. We'd only been out for three days. The whole tour was like that, one border-line catastrophe after another.

Farther along in the tour we played a gig in El Paso where we all got good and drunk after the show. Later that evening, I saw Mike Albert in a corner of the backstage area, threatening to use his martial arts skills on one of the security guards. It felt as if the tour was constantly on the brink of disaster, with partying and wild behavior the whole time. I loved it—it was great to be out of Los Angeles and actually touring. It defined us as a band.

Despite the mishaps, the band's mood was good, and a couple of remarkable things happened during the tour. At one point we were in a motel in Kansas, sitting around with some girls who were prepared to provide some affection, food, and beer. We were broke—and I mean genuinely flat broke, with no resources except what these fine girls were willing to shell out for us. The girls helped us buy a little barbecue so we could grill some meat out in the parking lot.

I remember Dave called Steve Sinclair, our artists & repertoire (A&R) person at Combat Records, and told him how broke we were. He said, "We have no money, our credit card is maxed out, and shows are either not happening or being canceled." Steve replied, "You guys just need to go home and get jobs." That, more than anything, put the fuel on the fire for us. We knew then that our days at Combat were numbered.

At the same time a booking agent named Andy Somers came on board with us, and offered to ensure that the remaining shows went ahead and that we would get paid. He became our booking agent for the next several years, through the Countdown to Extinction tour, and was largely responsible for getting us signed to Capitol Records a year after we hired him.

I was drinking and smoking but using much less coke and heroin. I'd learned that most road coke was usually pretty bad, and heroin was harder to come by, so there wasn't much use trying to score on tour. Besides, there was always some beer on the rider, and someone, somewhere would usually have weed. I wasn't strung out on smack, but the smokes and libations kept me going and I still had a good time.

When we came home off the tour, Mike Albert quit, and we were fine with that. He wasn't the right long-term fit for us anyway. He didn't play the guitar parts in a Megadeth fashion, although he played the part of the fourth member onstage well enough. Chris Poland returned after that. He was on methadone as a way of detoxing from heroin, so we knew he would be able to tour.

We spent the fall of 1985 rehearsing just south of L.A. in an old warehouse that had been turned into rehearsal rooms. I slept there a few times, and so did Dave, because we were essentially homeless. It was a landing pad where we could hang out, drink beers, and write a new record, which we called *Peace Sells . . . but Who's Buying?*

I remember Dave picking up my B.C. Rich Eagle bass, off of which I had ripped the frets and made it into a fretless, and composing a loose version of the introductory riff to the song "Peace Sells." We picked up Gar in Pasadena for rehearsal that night and while I was driving, Dave wrote the lyrics to that song. By the next day, the whole song was musically written. We already had "Devil's Island," and a bunch of the other songs were written pretty fast. The following year, it was an amazing thrill to hear my performance of the "Peace Sells" line as the intro to *MTV News.* They used it for something like ten years during that segment.

Dave and I were then living over in Echo Park, which is just east of Hollywood, close to Dodger Stadium. We rehearsed at a place called Mars Studios in East Hollywood, and I took a job there, eventually managing the place. It gave me an opportunity to sell pot out of there from time to time, because, like any good musician, I didn't want to get a job but needed to make money somehow. The idea was that we could take some of our merchandising advance money, buy some pot and sell it, and that would help us to continue to make more money. Of course, we made very little profit, because I became my own best customer.

The only real job I ever did in L.A. was selling appointments at the solar energy company, which I mentioned earlier. Eventually I realized that I didn't have time to work because I was too busy with the band, which was fine with me; the sacrifices would be worth it one day.

All this was happening as we were recording the *Peace Sells . . .* record. We were still essentially homeless. I'd even joined the Holiday Health Club at the corner of Sycamore and Hollywood Boulevard for a hundred dollars a month, so I'd have somewhere to shower each day. Chris had a wealthy girlfriend who was taking care of him. Gar was still working at B.C. Rich Guitars, so he had a good day job, although eventually he had to quit in order to go on tour. He started working for his girlfriend's father in carpentry to make money during his downtime.

Dave and I were the ones running Megadeth. He quarterbacked all the plays, of course, but I was the center or the wide receiver, essentially his vice president. It was always us doing the grunt work. We were the ones who made the lifestyle sacrifices to keep Megadeth alive.

Back home, my father was going through a lot of hardship with the farming business. He lost one of his farms and had to turn another one into the bank, because, like a lot of other farmers, he'd taken out high-interest-rate loans on expensive farmland a few years prior, when times were good. My mother went back to work as a caregiver at a nursing home in Jackson, and my father had to work out a way of handing the farm over to my brother so he could get out of farming. It was great that my brother was there to take over; it was unnecessary even to discuss my coming back to run it.

Dave knew a girl named Nancy whose friend Mercedes was a model for pornographic magazines. Mercedes took a liking to me and I moved in with her. Now I had a home, albeit a cockroach-infested hole in the wall. Mercedes once did a photo shoot with the legendary porn star John Holmes, and I thought, "Now I'm done for, I can't possibly compete with him!" But it all worked for me, because I had a place to live where I could do heroin and have a good time with her. She liked to do drugs and cocaine, too. My drug use really accelerated during this period because she had access to really high-quality Persian heroin, mostly from a local taxi driver who would deliver it right to our apartment in West Hollywood, just off Sunset Boulevard across from Tower Records.

Mercedes and I were an item, for no other reason than convenience, although later when I took an HIV test and the results were negative, I realized how lucky I'd been—and also how foolish. I fell for Mercedes, I genuinely did, but it turned out that she was doing private "escort" work on the side, which was too much heartbreak and reality for me. I later found out that this was a common form of income for a lot of the rock 'n' roll groupie girls in Hollywood—strip dancing, nude pinup magazines, and escort work.

Like most rock 'n' rollers, I didn't mind a bit of attention from groupies here and there. The women up in San Francisco were pretty tough broads, with leather jackets, attitude, and so on. Down in Los Angeles the women were much sexier, and more appealing to me. Then again, they weren't really into thrash metal; they were more into the Sunset Strip hair bands. There were always enough girls around, though.

It was all a rather different life for a Lutheran farm kid from Minnesota. I was naïve and an easy target, but also a willing participant. L.A. was like a great big adult playground where you could make up your own rules, which I tried to do, all the time realizing that these were not the morals and standards set down for me as a kid from the Midwest.

In January and February 1986, we did a short tour of the East Coast in a freezing motor home. It was technically the second leg of the Killing Is My Business . . . tour, even though we were already playing songs from *Peace Sells . . . but Who's Buying?* In many ways it was our form of preproduction for the record, performing those songs live each night. It was then that we realized we had something of a hit song with "Peace Sells." It really put some excitement in our lives to know that we were moving on to a more mature sound with these new songs, too. This was a sound that really became our own with the next album.

At our show at Irving Plaza in New York City, our booking agent Andy Somers brought down Tim Carr, the A&R talent scout from Capitol Records. Tim liked what he heard and within months offered us a contract with Capitol. Andy also hooked us up with his friend and manager Keith Rawls, who later assisted in our signing to Capitol Records and managed us from the *Peace Sells . . .* through the *So Far, So Good . . . So What!* records.

After that tour we started putting plans together to record *Peace Sells . . .* at the Music Grinder studio on Melrose Avenue in Hollywood. The recording was contractually still with Combat Records, our label at the time. We had a $25,000 budget from them this time, so we could put ourselves on small salaries. It also allowed us to bring in an outside producer, Randy Burns. He and his engineer Casey McMackin worked fast and furious on the album. Casey was an excited young lad who spent a long time running through guitar and bass tones with us and offering suggestions on parts and revisions—in many ways, responding like a producer.

Once the record was done, we turned it in to Combat, and Dave and I took a trip back to Minnesota to relax for a few days, because we were being courted by Elektra Records in New York City, who had previously signed Metallica. (This was just before Capitol Records put their offer out to us.) We stopped off at the farm in Minnesota and hung out there for about a week. It was weird to be back home, having been steeped in the L.A. drug lifestyle. I remember I brought some smack with me and I had to detox off the stuff while at my parents' home.

Once I was back on the farm, my dad—who had never been one to mince words—made it clear that he was a bit skeptical of our lackluster success. As much as he wasn't a music guy, he did understand show-business etiquette. He used to say to us, "You need to treat your fans better, stop swearing onstage, and start writing more mainstream songs!" I could tell this freaked Dave out, but he listened to my dad out of respect.

My father was like that: he earned your respect because he called it like he saw it, whether you liked it or not. It was an interesting dynamic to see my dad and Dave together, eating together and praying at the dinner table together. I think Dave really liked it. It was a different family dynamic from the one he knew, and very comforting when compared to our hand-to-mouth existence in L.A., building the band.

When we were in New York a few days later, it was game on once again. I was back to using and drinking. Dave and I shared a room at the Omni Hotel by Central Park, and our manager was giving us money to live on, which felt as if heaven had parted and given us some grace. The pressure was finally off and it felt like we really were going to have a future. It was there in New York that I was introduced to the drug ecstasy. I took it and asked what it was. That's how bad I'd gotten: I would take a drug and *then* ask what it was! I'd never taken it before, and I didn't feel anything until about thirty minutes later, when we got to the legendary club CBGB, down in the Bowery neighborhood of Manhattan. All of a sudden I started coming on to this new drug high. It was bizarre: really, really weird, like a mix of acid and cocaine—I was hyper but tripping. It was often used as an aphrodisiac.

I was high as a kite as we went club hopping around New York City. On the one hand it was like something you'd see in a movie, being wined and dined by a real major label with a promise of fame and fortune in front of you. On the other hand, I kept trying to sober up, thinking that I had to keep my wits about me and at least try to be a professional in the midst of all the partying. Fortunately, nothing happened beyond a great party, but it was a surreal event. We were treated like rock royalty and whisked in and out of the trendiest VIP clubs in town, with no questions asked. It was a buffet of drugs and girls, and it felt as if we'd made the big time.

On the way home from New York, I was thinking about my life in L.A. We'd actually had a home for that one week in New York, with all expenses paid by people who had real interest in us and could actually make things happen. I was hip to Mercedes's escort work and it was killing me.

Fortunately, not long after that New York trip, some more major labels started taking an interest in the band, and Capitol Records finally put an offer on the table, which in turn escalated to a bidding war with Elektra. Capitol won out. That released some record advance money to us at last, and our manager got the band a three-bedroom apartment over in Silverlake, just east of Hollywood. We had a home and a real band headquarters at last.

You always hope that you'll get a major deal when you're a musician. Metallica had paved the way for the thrash metal bands, and certainly the Big Four, as Metallica, Megadeth, Anthrax, and Slayer were later collectively known, by signing with Elektra back in the mid-1980s. Right after we signed with Capitol, Anthrax signed with Island Records, and Slayer signed with Def Jam. As a band, and even as a genre, we were finally starting to find our way.

A THOUGHT

Money

Sometimes you have to make the most critical decisions in life under excruciating circumstances. This has been the case for me many times. Financial decisions are hardest to make when you have no money. Moral decisions are likewise hard when you have no morals. I've been between a rock and hard place on these matters more than once in my career.

Fortunately, a good friend counseled me that when making career decisions I should ask myself, "What does the decision look like when I remove the financial reward? Is it still worth doing?" If not, I know that if I proceed I will really be doing it only for the money.

Finances come and go, but what's really important is whether you can truly leave your mark on an endeavor. If it is still worth doing with no monetary reward, then it is worth doing for a greater reason.

CHAPTER FIVE

Hitting Bottom

"You can't do the wrong thing the right way."

—Anonymous

There's one thing that I've always appreciated about Dave Mustaine: Megadeth was never about buddies sitting around jamming. It's a very focused mission, and Dave has the vision to achieve it. You meet him on his terms, not yours, and that dynamic works. Without him, the band wouldn't have its edge; without me, it would be complete gunfire at all times. The strategy of battle can't be constant surrender, but it can't be constant attack either. There has to be a little bit of both. He's the colonel and I'm the lieutenant, and between us we win the war. That sums up the dynamic between me and Dave, as it has from the very beginning of Megadeth.

When Capitol signed us, it felt like Megadeth was in big business. We visited the Capitol tower with our heads held high—even though when we left the tower, I went downtown to Ceres Street, scored some heroin, and took it back to our Silverlake apartment in small, rolled-up balloons, carrying them in my mouth to avoid getting busted.

Peace Sells . . . but Who's Buying? was released in the fall of 1986 and we were scheduled to start that tour with Motörhead down the west coast of California and the southwestern U.S. We hired designer Ray Brown to create some stage clothes for us, as he had designed looks for Judas Priest, Ratt, Mötley Crüe, and other big bands at that time. We did photo shoots and loads of media interviews around the new album, bought some new equipment, and quickly got our business up and running.

Motörhead were a notoriously tough bunch, like a biker gang. For this tour, their drummer, Pete Gill, had his kit set up on stage-prop train tracks, which came to the front of the stage and seriously impeded us in setting up our show with Gar's drums in the middle of the stage, and our amplifiers on each side. Dave was furious, and rightfully so, because we didn't have any stage space. That led to an argument between our manager, Keith Rawls, and Motörhead's manager just before the show at the Santa Monica Civic Auditorium, the second show of the tour. It seemed to me that both men puffed up their chests too much—and Keith pulled us from the last three dates of the tour.

Even now, I think that didn't need to happen. That decision to pull out of the tour led to a rift between Motörhead and Megadeth, which lasted until the Graspop festival in Belgium in 2001. Personally, I just wanted to play the bass and have a good time, but this was a power play between managers.

Lars Ulrich of Metallica came to see us on the first night of the tour at the Kaiser Center Auditorium in Oakland, California. He was pretty beat up, because it was right after Cliff Burton had died in the coach crash in Sweden. I asked Lars what he was going to do for a bass player, and he replied, "Why, do you want a job or something?" There was some speculation afterward about whether or not that was an offer, but I think it was simply rhetorical. They never formally approached me about the bass position. (In 2001, when Jason Newsted left Metallica, Dave told me that Lars had called him to get Dave's blessing for me to be on Metallica's list of bass players to consider. I didn't get the call, however.)

Cliff and Dave had remained friends after the split back in 1983. I didn't know Cliff well, but I thought he was very personable. He was a reserved, quiet guy, whereas Lars was very engaging and wanted to chat with whoever was in the room. When we got the news that Cliff had died in the crash, Dave was absolutely crushed. He wrote the music and lyrics for "In My Darkest Hour" that very day.

After the Motörhead dates we went out in support of Alice Cooper on his Constrictor tour, and the natural thing for us young bucks was to ask on a regular basis if we could meet Alice. Finally, one night after our set, we were told that he was ready to see us. We sobered up as best we could and went onto his bus. He was very cool: a very gentle, mellow guy. We got him onto the subject of partying, and he told us that he used to drink a bottle of whiskey a day—and that we needed to be careful so we wouldn't end up in a similar situation.

It was a quick conversation, but we were listening intently and there was a silence on the bus after he spoke. It was a sobering moment, and a clear reminder for me that I was blowing it with my drug and alcohol use. I knew I shouldn't be taking drugs, and it was as if the Good Lord had sent us a warning sign through Alice Cooper. If anyone knew the perils of addiction, it was he. Following the Constrictor tour, Alice and his organization made a big mainstream comeback with his next album. His words resonated with me, but I was too wrapped up in my addictions to take any action. Drugs are like that. The warnings to not start taking them can be helpful, but it's a whole different dynamic once you're already hooked.

Toward the end of the Peace Sells . . . tour, we agreed to record a song for the soundtrack of a forthcoming film called *Dudes*, starring Flea from the Red Hot Chili Peppers, Jon Cryer (later a star of the popular TV show *Two and a Half Men*), and Lee Ving from the punk band Fear. The film was directed by Penelope Spheeris. We recut our version of "These Boots" and it sounded great, partly because our chops were tight from being on the road.

This led to us appearing in Penelope's next film, *The Decline of Western Civilization Part II: The Metal Years*, which was part of our initial launch of the album, *So Far, So Good . . . So What!* in 1988. I was thrilled with the way we came across in our interviews, especially compared to most of the other musicians in the film. I talked a lot about integrity in my interview with Penelope, and I meant it, but I was extremely high on heroin when she recorded it. When I look at it now, it's obvious; my eyes give it away. I was completely hammered.

I used to pride myself on being a guy who could be pretty buzzed but not completely smashed. I rarely went over the top, although I remember one time I went up to the Rainbow Bar and Grill on Sunset Boulevard with Mercedes. She had given me a downer called Placidyl, and as we walked home, my legs gave out from under me. I collapsed right on Sunset Boulevard and just lay there laughing. The truth is, I was never that into pills. Heroin was more my thing, as it seemed to fuel my artistry. I loved playing bass on heroin, and the thought of giving it up terrified me. I wondered if I would ever enjoy playing without it.

In 1987, at the end of the Peace Sells . . . world tour, Chris was fired again, and we had to let Gar go, too. Chris was completely strung out and Gar was just hanging on. It was very sad: we'd had two records with this lineup. On the one hand, it was really hard for me to stand by that decision, because I was also doing drugs. It was hypocritical, but we believed it was in the best interests of the band. Gar had been doing heroin a lot longer than I had, and he was shooting up. I was not. Also, Dave and I were the metal guys in Megadeth; Chris and Gar were the jazz guys. They were a bit older and seemed less invested in the band than we were. Their thinking was more along the lines of "I need to make a living—do I have a career or not?" Dave and I were younger, hungrier, and had a lot less to lose.

After Chris's departure from Megadeth he went on to completely straighten out his life. In fact, he became an inspiration for my own sobriety only a couple of years later.

Chuck Behler was Gar's drum tech, and we asked him to step up and sit in for Gar when he didn't show up for a sound check at a show we had in Washington, D.C. Chuck sounded great, so we asked him to join the band in time to begin writing our third album, *So Far, So*

Good . . . So What! I was playing a lot of guitar by this time, as there were only three of us. The riff for "Hook in Mouth" was one of mine, as were parts of "Liar." The album was written and recorded very quickly, but we needed a second guitarist, which took a while to find.

First, we asked Jay Reynolds of Malice if he would join the band because he was a friend of mine, and he was someone Dave had known a little bit on the L.A. metal scene. Jay and I were casual party friends and had fun talking about our bands, going to the Rainbow to pick up girls, using drugs, and so on. He was a likable, fun-loving guy, but it became apparent very quickly that he didn't have the necessary style of guitar playing needed for Megadeth. We hadn't checked out his playing well enough before we gave him the green light to join us.

I was always the one who got new guys up to speed, for countless hours and days, getting them acquainted with the songs and the riffs. I would get them about 75 percent of the way there, and then Dave would take them up the rest of way. It was utility grunt work, but I was happy to do it. It stemmed from the work ethic I'd acquired as a kid, as well as my desire to see the band flourish. In the process, I learned a lot about the intricacies of the band's guitar style, too.

Jay Reynolds (Malice): I first met David while hanging out with Megadeth. I found out later that he and I were a lot alike. David was a guy who got things done, just as I had been that guy in my other band, Malice. We became fast friends and we've remained close over the years. We pick up right where we left off. He's a great guy: he and Dave Mustaine are unique characters. Guys like them are few and far between.

Jay suggested that he bring in his guitar teacher, Jeff Young, to record the solos on the album and then later show him how to play those solos. However, while Jeff was obviously a studied player, having graduated from the Guitar Institute of Technology in Hollywood, he was just as obviously not a heavy metal guitarist. Jeff did create some amazing solos and he played them himself on the record. He became our new guitarist shortly thereafter. I'm glad to say that Jay remained a good friend of mine afterward, in spite of the transitions.

Jeff turned out to be a fantastic guitar player. We often roomed together on the tour and he would show me a lot of things on the guitar. Effectively, I studied with him, and we made a good musical partnership.

Around this time, my heroin use really escalated and I was looking for options to get off the stuff. One of those was detox through methadone. But the other problem with methadone is that it is very addictive, and withdrawal from it is even worse than withdrawal from heroin. It also really hurt the arches of my feet for some reason. I would get out of bed in the morning and my feet would be in agony as they touched the floor. Some mornings I'd take methadone in an attempt not to take heroin, but then I'd get really tired, so I'd score some cocaine, and then I'd get so high on coke that I had to take heroin. So now I was on methadone, cocaine, *and* heroin!

Greg Handevidt (school friend):

I remember David telling me that his drug problems had got really bad, around the time that Megadeth recorded *So Far, So Good . . . So What!* I was surprised that it had gotten so bad in such a short time. You imagine a junkie as a dead-looking person who sort of wanders around, but David was never like that.

* * *

Jeff Young was friends with producer/engineer Michael Wagener, who mixed the *So Far . . .* record. I loved the sound of Michael's records in those days, but for some reason that production style didn't work so well on the *So Far, So Good . . .* record. I'd always been impressed with Michael's mix on Metallica's *Master of Puppets* album, but *So Far . . .* sounded nothing like that. Perhaps the Metallica guys were looking over his shoulder when he mixed *Puppets* to make sure it sounded right, with no reverb on the drums and so on. Michael was a good guy and a top-notch producer/engineer, but that record just didn't turn out the way we'd hoped.

By this time, Mercedes was out of my life. She had really broken my heart, and with all of our touring I was able to support myself, no longer relying on girls and their apartments to have a home. It was incomprehensible to me that anyone would do escort work to pay the bills, and highly dangerous. Oddly, and in spite of my lifestyle, I was always loyal to my girlfriends.

After the release of *So Far, So Good . . . So What!*, we traveled around the country and did a tour with Dio and Savatage. We played the Long Beach Arena, and I met a girl named Charlie there after the show. After being on the road for the better part of a year, I was ready to settle down with a girl at home. Charlie and I hit it off well, and pretty soon we moved in together into an apartment over in central Hollywood on Cherokee Street, just off Highland Avenue. She hated that I did drugs, so I did them in secret.

One night, Slash and Steven Adler from the up-and-coming Hollywood band Guns N' Roses came over to our apartment. They looked around and were like, "How did you get this?" The GNR guys had basically grown up on the streets of Hollywood, and here I was, having sold a couple of gold records. I didn't have a load of money, but I was a fairly together guy with a car and my bills paid. It was as if they were amazed that the guy from Megadeth could have a civilized home life.

A THOUGHT

Substance Versus Content

Life in a rock band is largely about selling perception, the rock star dream. Being homeless and completely broke for several years wasn't the dream I'd come to L.A. for, and it really changed me. The allure of Hollywood nightlife brings something hauntingly romantic to your life when you're woven into its fabric. For me, I was living the dream, but at the same time, two worlds were colliding: my passion for music and my enslavement to addiction.

CHAPTER SIX

Hollywood Nights

> "Sometimes the longest twelve inches are between the head and the heart."
>
> —Anonymous

Things got pretty crazy during the *So Far, So Good . . . So What!* tour period. I was at the party where Nikki Sixx of Mötley Crüe overdosed and died for a few minutes, a story he chronicled in his book *The Heroin Diaries*. Guns N' Roses' drummer Steven Adler had invited me over to the Franklin Plaza Hotel in Hollywood, where he and the band were staying at the time. He had broken his arm and wasn't playing during that period. However, GNR was playing a series of shows up in Pasadena and had hired drummer Fred Coury from Cinderella to fill in.

I went over to the Franklin Plaza with a friend of mine named Matt Freeman, an engineer over at Music Grinder studios. Matt had also worked as a studio assistant on *So Far, So Good . . . So What!* At one point, Slash and Nikki came barging into Steven's room, completely trashed out of their minds. I hadn't met Nikki before, and although we later became good friends, that night he was a real mess. Imagine a guy possessed by the devil when on drugs: that was Nikki. He had a look in his eyes that was terrifying. Nevertheless, I thought maybe they had some smack I could be dealt in on. No such luck. They eventually left our suite and went into the room next door and we carried on partying.

A short while later, a young woman partying next door came crashing into our room, saying, "Quick! Get some ice, Nikki overdosed." Fred frantically looked at me and said, "Dude, do you have a car? Get me out of here!" We immediately scurried out the door, just as the police and ambulance sirens began to wail. Matt and I took Fred over to the Hyatt Regency on Sunset Boulevard, which is also known as the infamous "Riot House." It's the hotel of legend where bands like the Who and Led Zeppelin built a reputation on excessive wild parties.

Fred wasn't a drug user; he just liked a couple of beers. He was a seasoned professional and said to me, "I do not need to be around any of this." I could tell he was mad about the situation and didn't want that kind of trouble in his life. Even though we were musically very different, Megadeth, Mötley Crüe, and GNR came from the same fabric of wild living, so I understood this evening in a demented sort of way.

Nikki was revived by the paramedics with a cardiac adrenaline shot. The next time I saw him, he was nine months sober, having been through rehab. He visited me during my first drug and alcohol rehab stint at the Valley Presbyterian Hospital in Van Nuys less than a year after the Franklin Plaza incident, an act of friendship I have never forgotten. He looked great: he was trim, because he was going to the gym, and he was calm and totally present. He had a very easy, natural, uplifting demeanor that was the polar opposite of the demon who had been at the Franklin Plaza with me just a few months earlier. He was a real testament to sobriety and its life-changing effects.

All in all, *So Far, So Good... So What!* was really the culmination of what had started in 1983: my transformation into a person that I really wasn't. I put so much dope and booze into myself that I behaved like a completely different person. Was I born with the mind of an addict? I don't know that I was. All I know is that after repeated use of these substances, I became addicted to them. I couldn't moderate it, because my body had become used to having this stuff in it, and I became dope-sick when I didn't have any. In effect, I was denying my true self and letting my addictions turn me into someone I was not.

My smack use continued, because compared to some of the guys I was hanging with, I could get high and keep it together. I would do a line of coke and keep a joint in the ashtray of my car, and still be able to drive over to see attorneys and business managers and have reasonable conversations with them. The other guys didn't keep it together as well as I did. That perpetuated the lie and made me the most deceitful kind of drug addict, because you couldn't really spot it in me, especially when I stood next to others who were faring much worse.

My moral compass was pretty skewed at this point, too. I'd become very sneaky. When I thought someone in the room was holding on to some dope, I simply gave the nod or the look and asked, "Hey, are you holding?" All I had to do from there was the little handover, and then I'd sneak off to the bathroom and snort up a line.

When I went out on the road and couldn't score any heroin, I knew I'd be dope-sick from the withdrawal, so I'd drink myself to oblivion to dull the suffering. Off the road, I would go to downtown L.A., where I could buy heroin and cocaine out of a hotel-room window on Ceres Street. On the road, I could control my addiction, but at home, I couldn't. This type of lunacy couldn't last, though. A turning point was coming, and it finally arrived when we went to England.

In June 1988 Megadeth was booked to play at the Monsters of Rock festival in Donington, England, one of the most prestigious festivals in the world at that time, and a high point of our careers to date. A few days before our flight, a friend called me while my girlfriend Charlie and I were lying in bed. I thought Charlie was still asleep, and my friend asked me, "Hey man, you got any dope? Can I get some from you?"

After I hung up the phone, Charlie said, "I heard that! What's going on here?" She freaked out, went into the bathroom, and found my stash of brown Persian heroin—which she dumped all over the brown carpet in our living room. I knew then that I was going to be really dope-sick in about half an hour. Even worse, she called my parents and told them, "David's on heroin!"

Now the cat was really out of the bag. My parents were terribly shocked. My father was especially upset. He'd really supported me and my chosen path of music, and he'd warned me on many occasions about drugs, girls, and anything else that could get in the way of my dream. "Don't do anything stupid and mess this up," he would tell me. "You've got a shot at something."

The flight to England was two or three days away, and I was dope-sick. Charlie wouldn't let me go anywhere without her, so I couldn't sneak out and score. It was horrible. She gave me an ultimatum, saying that if I wanted to be with her, I would have to go to rehab at Van Nuys hospital after the trip to Donington.

Sobriety was already in the air in 1988. Bear in mind that at this time Aerosmith had gotten sober, as had the Mötley Crüe guys. Veteran musicians from the 1960s and '70s like David Crosby were sober, as were musicians and actors from all genres. Everybody was going public about getting sober, and the entertainment industry was excited about this new lifestyle of clean living. Furthermore, we had recently acquired new managers at McGhee Entertainment, Doc McGhee and his partner Doug Thaler. They told me, "If you want to get sober, we'll help you, we've got the right people," but they also made it real clear to me that they weren't going to drag incapacitated people around the world anymore. "We're done with it," they said. "We're not going through that anymore."

While the managers and labels were embracing sobriety for their artists, I was like, "This sobriety movement is way ahead of my time!" I was a kid from a farm in Minnesota and, having found all this sex, drugs, and rock 'n' roll, I was thinking that I'd made it. Now was the time to let the candle burn! I'd seen the *Sid and Nancy* movie where Sid is asked by Nancy's father what his goals are in life, and Sid answers, "I think I'll move to Paris and go down in a blaze of glory." That was how Megadeth lived, to some degree: we were about lighting the fuse and letting it burn until the explosion.

We flew from L.A. to New York and played at the Ritz on our way to England as a warm-up show. I was able to get some dope and "get well," as we called it, so that little two-day trip was fine. Charlie met me in New York and flew with me to London, and of course, you can get as high as you want *before* you get on a plane. I managed to stay as high on smack as I could, for no other reason than I knew the inevitable was coming.

We arrived in England and drove up to the show in Leicestershire. The Guns N' Roses guys had just gotten there, and I thought they might have some drugs, but they were like me in that when they were at home in L.A. they might be a mess, but on the road their partying was restricted to drinking. No one had any smack. The inevitable detox, which I knew would be painful, was coming at a moment in time when I needed to be at my best for the biggest show of my life. So I went to our hotel, the Holiday Inn in Leicester, and became so sick that everybody found out about it. Many of them were angry because I had lied about my addiction, but they also knew that inside I was a good kid, and their concern trumped their anger.

The insidious nature of drug addiction is that while you're reaching out for help with one hand, you're reaching out to your dealer with the other. A doctor came up to the hotel and gave me a prescription for some codeine aspirin, which did nothing for me. But he had no sympathy. "You junkie American!" he said in disgust.

The next day I somehow played the Donington set—the biggest show of my life, in front of 107,000 people—but I was so sick and strung out, I was dying up there. Onstage, I violently whipped myself around, using the adrenaline to distract me from the pain. Once I got off the stage, I was so sick that I just went to the bus and fell apart, hearing KISS in the distance as we rolled back to the hotel for the night.

Right after Donington, we had three more stadium festival shows scheduled with Iron Maiden in Germany, and I ended up having to cancel Megadeth's participation in all three of them so I could go home and get into rehab, as Charlie and I had agreed. Our agent, while very shocked, stood by me. I don't know who was responsible for making up my excuse, which was that I'd broken my arm in the shower and had to cancel the shows, but I wanted to take the blame for the cancellations somehow, even if I didn't want it said that "David Ellefson's on heroin and has to go to rehab." I wasn't quite ready for that yet.

Nowadays, of course, everyone can talk about rehab, because our culture is used to celebrities crashing and burning. Back then, it wasn't in vogue yet. It was horrible and embarrassing. I've since gone back and tried to make it right with everybody, because I put people in a position where they had to lie to cover for me. That's probably the worst part of addiction: You may think you're going out in a blaze of glory by yourself and that your life is your own. You simply want to be left alone to do what you want. But the reality is that you're connected to other people and you're taking some of their moral character down into the flames with you. Everyone around the addict suffers, too.

We flew home to Los Angeles and I went straight into a drug rehab program at the Valley Presbyterian Hospital, with the help of the sobriety guru Bob Timmons, who had been recommended to me by our management. It was supposed to be a ten-day detox, but I only lasted three. Quite early on in treatment they told me, "David, there's only one thing you have to change, and that's everything," which was scary. I thought, "You know what? No girlfriend is worth this much suffering." I left and scored dope to get high on my way home.

Charlie bailed pretty quickly after that.

Although my first stint in rehab had failed, I was still going to methadone clinics in L.A., trying to get sober—or at least trying to get off heroin, which is not the same thing. At the same time, we were demoing songs for our next album, which would become Rust in Peace, including "Holy Wars . . . the Punishment Due," "Tornado of Souls," and "Rust in Peace . . . Polaris."

We had a rehearsal room over by Dodgers Stadium, a decrepit little hole of a place called the Hully Gully. Dave, Chuck, and I would rehearse there every night. Usually I'd wake up at about three or four in the afternoon, get some dope, and start rehearsing by seven or eight o'clock. I'd be up until five or six in the morning. I started when the sun went down and passed out shortly after the sun came up. I was a total vampire.

Despite our writing songs for *Rust in Peace*, these were really our darkest days. I wanted to clean up, but I wasn't ready. I didn't want my current life, but I didn't know if I wanted a new life either. I was just dying somewhere in the middle, with one foot in tomorrow and one foot in yesterday, oblivious to the beauty of today.

Slash from Guns N' Roses often came over to hang with Dave and me around this time, as GNR were just wrapping up their world tour for *Appetite for Destruction*. We had a good time together, just playing guitar, partying, and thoroughly enjoying ourselves. It was funny because I would play a lot of guitar with Slash and it felt like a really creative period, but Dave would just look at us and say, "You guys just play the same riff over and over again. . . ."

Slash was a great guitar player and a supercool guy. It was a real treat to jam with him. He really understood metal music, but was also a very broad-based rock 'n' roll guitarist, with a gutsy vibe to his playing. With the successful completion of the Appetite for Destruction tour, the financial floodgates were about to open up huge for GNR, but at this time he was still living in a tiny, one-bedroom apartment right behind Tower Records on Sunset Boulevard. There was a lot of chatter along the lines of "What would it be like if Slash came into Megadeth?" but that was really about it.

I still had to deal with my ongoing drug habit. My first attempt at rehab had failed, so I checked myself into Brotman Medical Center in Culver City in February of '89. During that stay I experienced a brief moment of clarity. There was a big hall there where they always had their Saturday-night meeting, and it was mandatory for all the rehab patients. I was so dope-sick and strung out that it felt like having the flu, mono, and pneumonia all at once. One night at the mandatory meeting, the evening's speaker was talking right in front of me. I was a few rows back, and I just bowed my head to pray and asked, "God, please stop me from feeling so bad right now." A few minutes later I realized that I was actually paying attention to the speaker and I was no longer thinking about myself and how terrible I felt. I remember it clearly: I prayed, I asked for help, and I got an instant result—even if it was fleeting. It was my first spiritual experience since I was fourteen.

I still didn't want to be sober; I just didn't want to be strung out anymore. I didn't want to change my life, because I was scared of leaving my comfort zone, even though it was actually quite uncomfortable. As a result, that second rehab didn't work, nor did a third attempt the following month. I kept hearing at meetings that half measures avail you nothing, that you're either all in or you're all out—it's that simple. Besides being strung out, I was running out of money, accruing debts, and unable to pay my bills. I was really living on borrowed time on every level—financially, spiritually, and morally.

During this period in 1989 we had to make a drummer change with Chuck Behler, who had recorded and toured *So Far, So Good . . . So What!* His drum tech Nick Menza was always brought in on that tour as an understudy for Chuck, in case anything ever happened to him and we needed a replacement behind the drum kit. Dave told me to check him out, so I went over and auditioned Nick at a small rehearsal hall just west of the Burbank Airport in the San Fernando Valley.

Nick was a very charismatic guy and quite artistic, too. He liked to draw and he could play guitar fairly well when writing his own songs. His father was a renowned jazz bebop sax player named Don Menza. If you mentioned his name in jazz circles, people really lit up. Nick was really excited when he auditioned for the band, and he looked great behind the drum kit. He talked fluent "dude" and was the Tommy Lee of thrash metal.

Once Nick was in the band, we started guitar auditions to round out the new lineup. We tried the guy from Jag Panzer and a bunch of others, some of whom had prepared and some who had not. Some of them assumed that they would get the gig without knowing that many of the nuances in Megadeth's music are found in the picking hand, not just the fingerboard hand. A lot of guys learned the notes for the fretting hand, but never understood the rest until they got in the room with us. Other musicians, however, understood the advanced techniques behind our music.

Mike Kroeger (Nickelback): Ellefson's bass playing is incredible, because the style of music his band plays requires him to play really intricate parts. I've learned a few of the songs that Dave Mustaine writes, and they're really hard—yet Ellefson nails them perfectly.

Dave, Nick, and I had this understanding that the guy would set up next to me in the auditions, because I was, as it were, the band's de facto diplomat. I'd help him set up and then Dave would call the tunes. We could tell within the first four to eight measures of a song whether there was a vibe: it was that quick. It's like being with a girl— you pretty much know within the first few sentences of the conversation whether or not you click. Dave and I had a secret message where we would reach back and switch off the wireless transmitter packs on our guitars, and we'd know right then that the audition was over. Then Nick would be the guy to usher him out the door. We met half a dozen guitarists. I was usually the one who would have to tell them that it hadn't worked out.

"Dimebag" Darrell Abbott of Pantera was invited to audition around this time. Back when I was dating Charlie, we went to visit her parents in Texas. During that trip, she suggested we make time to hang out with the guys from Pantera. I guess she'd dated Dimebag or something. He was called "Diamond" Darrell back then, and he was a big guitar star in the magazines. Pantera were the reigning champions of Texas back then, but they were still a hair band, having just gotten Phil Anselmo in the band and recorded their *Power Metal* album. We did some drinking with them and Darrell told me, "Man, *Peace Sells* . . . changed my life." The next night we went to hear them play at a club in Dallas. They were great: it was mostly cover songs, with a few originals, too. They invited me to join them onstage to play "Peace Sells" with them. They played great, even though they drank hard.

I told Dave about this in early 1989 when we started putting out feelers for guitar auditions, and brought up Dime's name. Pantera were just turning the corner, though, because they were about to sign to Atco and were ready to record *Cowboys from Hell*.

We also considered Jeff Waters of Annihilator. Nick and I were huge Annihilator fans, but Jeff was in a very different headspace in those days with Annihilator coming quickly up the ranks. So it never went anywhere. In recent years I've become good friends with Jeff, and we've talked about the "what-ifs" had he joined the band. He's a great guy and I love hanging with him.

We'd just about given up. Dave and I had moved to a new apartment complex called the Studio Colony over in Studio City, and by then I was quite strung out. I would wake up at three or four in the afternoon after the previous night's partying, having missed my 1 P.M. call time for rehearsal. Nick was on time and often waited hours for us to show up. Despite all this, we had demoed three songs over at Track Record Studios back when Chuck Behler was still in the band, and these served as the foundation of the new album. They were

"Tornado of Souls," "Polaris," and "Holy Wars." We spent our time auditioning guitarists and writing the rest of the record. Nick was the only successful audition out of the batch, so the three of us soldiered on.

During this time I was on various methadone programs, and I would have to drive about thirty to forty-five minutes in rush-hour traffic from the San Fernando Valley to Hollywood to get it, because the clinic only offered it between six and ten o'clock in the morning. If you missed those hours, you were sure to be dope-sick.

I'd started having serious emotional and mental breakdowns from doing so much cocaine. I recall one night in particular, I called Nick and his girlfriend Stephanie after I'd had a load of cocaine, even though everyone thought I was clean, and I was all nervous about it. I freaked out, left a rambling message on Nick's answering machine, and flushed all the cocaine down the toilet in a drug-induced panic. The next day, when Nick and Stephanie asked me if everything was all right, I tried to cover my tracks and make out like everything was cool. Talk about shame.

As I said earlier, sobriety was a big trend at the time. One day I was sitting in my apartment waiting for my drug dealer to call and the phone rang. It was Steven Tyler of Aerosmith. He had called, at the urging of Bob Timmons, to make a sobriety call on me. It was basically one addict reaching out to share his testimony with another addict. I understood why he was calling, and I'd grown up as a big fan of Aerosmith. Now, as a professional contemporary, I really grasped the purpose of the call. But as I was sitting there, I was thinking to myself, "Man, I can't believe I'm sitting here listening to my idol telling me to get off drugs, and at the same time I have to hurry him up and get him off the phone so my drug dealer can call me!" All my childhood dreams were being blocked by my addiction. That was the whole of 1989 for me, hiding and sneaking around to feed my addiction.

Around this time we switched managers to Ron Laffitte, who really helped the band by bringing us some great new opportunities.

Ron Laffitte (former Megadeth manager): I already knew the members of Megadeth from my years on the California heavy metal scene. I took over their management during the *So Far, So Good . . . So What!* campaign, when they all seemed to have spun out of control. David Ellefson was critical to the balance of the band. As intense as Dave Mustaine was, David was measured, calm, and low-key. He always seemed to be in complete control, despite the fact that he was suffering from drug stuff like the rest of them. He always seemed to be focused and conscious and attentive, and he always showed up, which was very comforting to me, especially in the early days, when I was transitioning into taking over the band's management. I'd show up for a meeting or a rehearsal, and no one else would be there except for David. He may have been using, or he may have been jonesing and in really bad shape, and I wouldn't even know it.

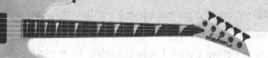

Throughout that year, I tried to maintain the illusion of sobriety by attending a few meetings, taking appointments with a drug counselor, and even picking up sobriety celebration chips for thirty, sixty, and ninety days clean. The truth was, just before each chip I had actually lapsed back into drug use, even if just for a day. I remember sitting in my apartment and thinking, "This is a real drag. Everybody thinks I'm sober. I don't have a girlfriend anymore and I can't even invite anybody over to get high, because they all think I'm sober!" So a month went by and I got high. Then a second month went by and the same thing happened, and I didn't tell anybody—so everybody thought I was three months sober, when really I only had a month because I'd slipped every month for three months in a row. It was embarrassing, and I realized how powerless I really was against my addiction.

My conscience was kicking in, big time. Lots of people who thought of me as a junkie had distanced themselves because I couldn't be trusted. There is a saying, "A belly full of booze and a head full of recovery is a pretty awful feeling," and that was exactly where I was in life. I knew what sobriety looked like, but I just couldn't bring myself to seize it. It was like swinging from a vine in the jungle but being too afraid to let it go and grab the next vine in front of me. I was stuck.

Then, in the summer of 1989, Ron Laffitte introduced us to Desmond Child, who was an A-list songwriter for artists like Bon Jovi and other major arena rock stars. He was hired to produce our single "No More Mr. Nice Guy," a cover version of the famed Alice Cooper song, intended for inclusion in the soundtrack for the film *Shocker*. This was the first song we recorded with Nick Menza. At the time, I hated the song, though I don't dislike it now. Not so much the actual song itself, but because of the way the whole process was handled businesswise with people around the band. It felt as if it should really have been a Dave Mustaine solo song rather than a Megadeth tune.

Meanwhile, I was plummeting further still into the pit of my addiction. Rehab hadn't worked, methadone hadn't worked, and the last vestige of something I was holding on to, which was my identity in Megadeth, was threatened because my senior partner told me that if I got high I'd be out of the band. The one thing I was holding on to was the "Hey, it's rock 'n' roll" attitude, where I could just take drugs, party with the girls, get onstage, and still feel validated. The bad news about rock 'n' roll is that it is very forgiving of decadence; it actually celebrates that way of life.

Ron Laffitte wanted to help me get sober, and he really did help me, just when I needed it most. I remember bursting into tears in front of him one day in the apartment in Studio Colony, when I was suffering most, and telling him that I needed help. He said, "If you want help, I can get it for you—but you have to really want to quit drugs for this to work." I said, "Yes, I really want to quit." He then introduced me to a doctor in Hollywood who prescribed a medication called Buprenex. You'd inject it into your buttock with a diabetes needle and it would curb the heroin withdrawal symptoms. That was the beginning of the end of my addiction, but I wasn't out of the woods quite yet.

Ron Laffitte (former Megadeth manager): I've never used drugs in my life, so when I became Megadeth's manager I thought it was important to learn about drug abuse and the behavior that surrounds it. As a result, I spent a lot of time educating myself and going to Al-Anon meetings. I met a couple of sobriety experts in the music business: Bob Timmons, who helped sober up various rock musicians; Tim Collins, who was Aerosmith's manager and became a mentor to me; and John B., who played a central role in helping David become sober.

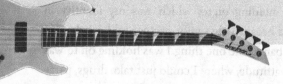

I now had a professional counselor helping me, a guy named John B., and I started working through the sobriety process with him. He was a former addict who was five years sober with the recovery programs, and he was doing some one-on-one and group counseling on the side.

Do you want to know how I finally got sober? It went like this: By November 1989, I was in deep trouble with my addiction but starting to use this Buprenex. I'd been through several methadone detox programs throughout 1989, none of which worked, because I'd do the methadone and I'd get so high that I realized that I needed to go get some cocaine—and then when I got some cocaine I realized that it was twelve o'clock at night, and that I needed to get some heroin to come down, so I could get some methadone from the clinic. My opiate addiction had really progressed rather quickly, and I desperately needed help.

So, in early November I went to a party for *RIP*, a hard rock magazine owned by Larry Flynt's publishing company. I came home after the party, and I just couldn't get high anymore. Nothing was working for me. I had hit bottom, so I lay on my bed and I prayed: "Please, God, help me. I'm completely through." I knew I couldn't do it on my own anymore, and so I reached out to God. That was the last night I ever drank, and I only chipped on smack a couple more times over the next two months.

Suddenly, and with increasing frequency, thoughts of faith would come to me. I prayed often and started reading spiritual books, which was also when I began to develop my own concept and my own definition of God. I didn't know who I was praying to at first, but my prejudices toward religion had been softened after a visit to church with my dad during Christmas that year. I listened to the sermon and something clicked; my bias against religion melted away and I suddenly felt hope.

Then a strange thing happened. I'd been praying during this time— "God, help, help, help!"—and in quick succession, my two main smack connections got busted and went to prison. It felt as if God was doing for me what I couldn't do for myself. The way was being cleared and my temptations were stripped away.

Just as much, prayer seemed to be opening doors in other areas of my life, too. The guitar auditions finally paid off when Dave and I went up to Ron Laffitte's office one day, and sitting on his desk was a Cacophony album and Marty Friedman's solo album. Ron told us that Marty wanted to audition for Megadeth, and we said, "Is that Marty Friedman from the band Hawaii?" and he said it was. We agreed to the audition and set it up. Marty was very professional, bringing a guitar tech to come in and set up his gear for him. Marty was wearing white hi-tops and skin-tight black jeans with holes in them like the Ramones, a Ramones T-shirt, and a leather jacket: he looked like a rock star. A poor rock star, but a rock star nonetheless. He played really well. He understood the nuances of our music and played the songs perfectly.

Marty Friedman (former Megadeth guitarist): That audition felt really natural, as if the other three guys in the band were my high school buddies. There were no awkward silences or anything: it was just like, "Let's jam!" and it sounded really good. Mustaine delegated Ellefson to show me the songs: he really helped me a lot, especially at the beginning. I was stoked that he could play guitar as well as bass, because it made it real easy for me to transition into the band. I was very excited to be in a band whose music I loved so much.

We agreed that Marty was our guy. I did some initial woodshedding with him as I had done with everybody else. Nick had a friend who filmed all the guitar auditions, including Marty's, and we gave all those films to Capitol with the idea of doing a behind-the-scenes-with-Megadeth movie, but Capitol disposed of them. I was told that they threw them in a Dumpster and that a guy who was painting the building at the time pulled them out. They're all over YouTube now, of course. It's still fun to watch them all these years later.

We were now getting ready to go in and start recording *Rust in Peace*. The band and the producer, Mike Clink, showed up at the studio every day, recording the beginnings of *Rust in Peace* with the bass and drums and some of Marty's guitar tracks.

Jimmy Bain of Dio, whom I'd become good friends with from the tour in 1988, loaned me a Yamaha eight-string bass, and one day while playing in my apartment I came up with "Dawn Patrol." It's interesting how different instruments inspire you to play and write differently. Mike Clink, Nick, and I put down all the bass and drums and I recorded "Dawn Patrol." Dave had to choose between my song and one that Nick had written, and though he liked Nick's song, he preferred mine, so "Dawn Patrol" ended up on the album. It has the only mellow interlude of the entire *RiP* record.

By then Dave had quit smoking cigarettes. He was on a health kick, so I tried to quit, too. Right about this time the Federal Aviation Administration had decreed that there would be no more smoking on airplanes, and I thought, "Oh no! As a traveling rock 'n' roller, this is gonna be a real drag!" There was a place in Beverly Hills which treats cigarette withdrawal just like it was a drug withdrawal. They gave me a shot in the neck of some mind-altering substance, and a shot in the arm, which was a nicotine blocker, plus some scopolamine patches, and they told me, "Go home, throw out your ashtrays, and wash your clothes: you're a nonsmoker when you leave here." I was completely hammered on whatever this medication was. I remember being in the car with Nick and Marty while Dave was driving and they were all laughing at me because I was out of my mind on this dope that the clinic had given me.

But those drugs helped me get off Buprenex that week, and after that stop-smoking clinic I never did another drug again. I never have, to this day. That was the last week of February 1990, which is why I call March 1, 1990, my first day of sobriety. It was the beginning of true freedom from my addictions.

A THOUGHT

G.O.D.: Good Orderly Direction

My experiences show that I tried to live my life according to my own self-serving methods during the years of my addictions, only to find myself entrenched in them. Eventually they became a lifestyle that I couldn't stop or escape on my own.

When I became overwhelmed by my addictions, I realized that I had two choices. One was to go on to the bitter end, hoping blindly that one day things would magically be different. Or I could surrender to some higher power and trust it to pull me out of my dilemma. This sounds easy, but it isn't. However, when I was out of options, the right choice became clearer by the moment.

I was in a drug rehab back in 1989, during one of my darkest periods of heroin addiction. Some things changed quickly once I found sobriety. But not everything changed all at once. Rather, my new life developed over the course of many years.

What aided me in these life transitions was a concept I heard about at meetings, a cute little saying that somehow traveled the longest twelve inches, those being from my head to my heart. I was struggling with the God idea, but I heard it said that I should simply consider God as G.O.D. or "Good Orderly Direction." It was suggested that I pray to God, even if I didn't believe in Him, and then do the next right thing that was put in front of me. In other words, I should stop trying to control everything and trust that whatever the outcome was, it was God's will.

Regardless of what we each may call it, that concept of G.O.D. kept it simple for me, and the God idea really started to work in my life.

CHAPTER SEVEN

New Beginnings

"Do not conform to the patterns of this world."
—Romans 12:2

For any alcoholic or addict to get sober is really a remarkable act of grace. That is the spiritual connection. The moment you surrender your life and everything you do to a higher power, whether you understand that power or not, and you say, "My way isn't working: I've been beat," something happens in that moment and a sort of peace comes over you. To me, that is the presence of God—G.O.D., or Good Orderly Direction, as I now know it.

As we sober up and become more developed in our faith, we realize that the only successful life is a constant surrender of our human tendency of self-will. That is naturally inherent in all of us, something that is correctly adjusted in a normal person but is very maladjusted in an addict or alcoholic. Whether it's that way from the beginning, or it just turns that way as we decline in our drug and alcohol abuse, that lifestyle starts to bend our souls and our morality, and forces us to compromise everything that we know to be good, right, and wholesome. On that journey toward the bottom, our whole moral compass is completely skewed.

In February 1990, that was the point I had finally reached. It's known as hitting bottom. That is the feeling you have inside, and it does not depend on how much money you have in the bank, or whether you still have your family, job, or any status in this world. It depends on nothing whatsoever, because it's about your soul.

For me, that point came when I was still in Megadeth and I still had some income and status, although I hadn't paid my taxes in two or three years. Not because I hadn't made any money, but because I'd spent all my money on drugs. When I got sober I looked at my tax bill, and I could barely afford to pay the interest on what I owed.

There was a defining moment in March when I was one month sober and the only one around really giving sobriety an honest go. Suddenly some close friends and running buddies started to slip and use drugs again. It was frightening because I was faced with the stark realization that either I was staying sober for my friends or staying sober for myself.

I'm so glad that I had that moment, because in a nutshell that's what staying sober these past twenty-three years has been about. It's what I say to myself on a daily basis: my sobriety is numero uno. Even ahead of my family and career, because if I don't have sobriety, everything else will go away. Under sobriety come a lot of blessings, like being married, having a job—and mine is playing the bass—and having children.

The day I married my wife, Julie, I grabbed her hand and I prayed, because I knew that by myself I'd mess it up. I really felt that I needed to give our marriage to God. It was the same when my son, Roman, was born. I'll never forget the day. I was driving up 104th Street, which is right by where we lived in Scottsdale, Arizona, and the epiphany hit me that Roman was not our kid, he's God's kid, and has been entrusted to us. This requires stewardship of our time, our money, and our resources. Everything that had been given to us was to be used to raise Roman and, later, my daughter, Athena. Ultimately they are here to perform whatever duty for which the Lord has put them here.

These are just a few of the lessons I have learned since getting clean in 1990—but at the time, the struggle was far from over. Here was Marty Friedman, for example, joining Megadeth. He was excited musically and on every other level. He came in when the whole ship was just turning in an entirely new direction. It was a good direction, and the right direction, but here we were, sitting in our living rooms doing these counseling sessions, and Marty's going, "Dude, I just wanted to come in and play guitar—I didn't know I was going to have to bite off all this drama!"

Marty got involved with a lot more than he'd ever bargained for. He came up with the phrase "Megadeth: it is what it is, and it ain't what you thought it was going to be." This meant that there is a whole lot more to being a big rock band than just playing the notes and hitting the stage, especially with newfound sobriety in the camp. It was cool, though, because he'd been around and he had a bit of a fan following himself. Plus he had plenty of credibility as a guitar player. It was nice for us not to have to groom somebody from the start, especially when we had toured the world and were about to make our fourth album.

So now Megadeth was still made up of the two Daves and the two new guys, but we all looked the same and we thought the same. We listened to the same kind of music. Marty was from a small town in Maryland and I was from a small town in Minnesota, so we had grown up on a lot of the same kind of music. Marty had the theory that you either liked KISS and Black Sabbath or you liked Led Zeppelin and Aerosmith. Marty and I were both from the first camp, whereas Dave and Nick were more from the second. So we all fit in the band, which I think is why it became the favored Megadeth lineup for so many years. It looked, sounded, and felt right.

Marty Friedman (former Megadeth guitarist): We recorded *Rust in Peace* and went straight out on tour. Everybody was getting along really well, and everyone was on the straight and narrow. I liked that, because I hadn't been a drug person since I was in junior high. By the time I entered the band I hated anything to do with drugs. We worked long hours, and it was pretty intense: I had no idea it was going to be like that, but it was great.

It's amazing to realize now that we wrote *Rust in Peace* completely out of our minds on very hard drugs during 1988 and '89, but then got all sobered up in 1990 to record it, which meant that the execution of it was note-perfect. Also, the tempos were at breakneck speed.

Since then, all of the years that followed have been the best of my career. In rehab they said to me, "Try this sober way of life for a year. If you don't like it, we'll gladly refund all your misery." I remember coming up to a year of sobriety in March 1991 and I knew I wouldn't trade it for anything. There were still a few bumps in the road from time to time, but I was in a much better place than I was a year before.

When we started the Rust in Peace tour, I didn't have a credit card and I owed almost $80,000 in back taxes. I lived on twenty dollars in cash per day, because all of my tour salary went to pay my debts. I still had an apartment, though, and I had managed to buy a car before everything went bad for me with drugs. Fortunately, we had a new business manager who had restructured everything internally with the band.

Rust in Peace made Number 23 on the *Billboard* chart. It was like *Peace Sells . . . but Who's Buying?* in that it was recorded after a complete retooling of the band. We hadn't just replaced a couple of guys: we'd renewed the band from the ground up. We were sober and we had a different set of marching orders for ourselves and for everyone around us, including our manager and our business manager. We'd transitioned from being a partnership to being an actual professional corporation. I'd made enough mistakes and squandered enough money along the way to know what not to do, and sometimes that's one of the best hands you can be dealt in life because we often learn more from our mistakes than our victories.

This whole period was a lot of hard work. I was still completely broke. When you go to the record company and borrow money so you can use it as tour support and go out on the road, usually that money is 100 percent recoupable against your album's future sales. Even if you sell half a million records and you make $1.25 per record, an album usually costs a couple of hundred thousand to make, plus you usually shoot a couple of videos, which are at least 50 percent recoupable against your future royalties. If you borrow even more for tour support, you can see that your record royalties don't go very far even on a fairly decent-selling record.

It's like any business, in that it takes money to make money, and one thing that the general public doesn't understand about the music business is that when the Internet changed the record industry in the 2000s, it basically took away the capital resources that artists need in order to be able to do what they do. I was really lucky to have gotten in under the wire, back in the mid-'80s when we signed with Capitol, because we got to spark up this beast called Megadeth with the proper artillery—banking, marketing, sales, and manufacturing—that we needed from a major label. We weren't rich by any means, but we had a resource to draw from, at least.

Songwriting and publishing soon became a bone of contention in Megadeth. At first we agreed to split everything four ways. Dave got

Mike Kroeger (Nickelback):

I remember Ellefson came out to a gig and brought me some gear and made sure I was happy with everything. After the show he was hanging out in the parking lot with my brother Chad, and they each had an acoustic guitar—and Ellefson shreds! He's a monster on guitar. He could easily have been playing guitar in Megadeth, because he has all the parts nailed. How these guys can even move while they're playing this stuff is beyond me.

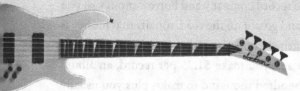

the publishing for the songs that he wrote, and of course those songs were and remain the heart and soul of Megadeth. I started to compose, and was credited and compensated on *So Far, So Good . . . So What?* for "Hook in Mouth," "Mary Jane," "In My Darkest Hour," and "Liar," which I composed on guitar, a much easier instrument for me to write riffs on than the bass. I never rated myself as a lead singer or a lead guitar player, but I've always been a pretty solid bass player and rhythm guitarist. In the early days we used a lot of Dave's publishing money to pay the bills, and eventually he got very protective of it. This was not unreasonable, and it served to inspire me to write, although money is never the best reason to write music.

One of our major challenges was how to keep Megadeth sober on the road. We called the tour managers and told them to remove all the alcohol from the minibars in the hotel rooms, to shield us from temptation. We also had a security guy who took care of us, although it should be noted that if an addict is determined to get high, he'll get through any security guy. I'll never forget flying to Amsterdam for a show and looking out of my hotel window to see people smoking heroin off tinfoil in the alley below. I thought, "Where were these people when I was getting high? Now they're right outside my window!" But I didn't stumble: I maintained my prayer life and recovery disciplines when I was traveling, and still do.

I was still full of anger and hostility, though. I was a very raw, exposed nerve. In fact, when I see old videos of myself I can see just how angry I was. I started to apply a recovery program in my life, but there is a saying, "Twenty miles in, twenty miles out," which is to say that you don't get sick with addiction overnight, so you probably won't become cured overnight either. I've never relapsed in all my time sober, because through prayer I think that part of me was removed. It just never came back. I'm lucky.

The day you start getting loaded is the day you stop growing emotionally—if you're an addict, at least. I started getting loaded when I was fifteen, so there I was on the Rust in Peace tour, a twenty-five-year-old teenager. And I behaved that way. I treated women as if I was fifteen, and my general responses to life were those of a fifteen-year-old. I was still growing up. I really felt that I'd turned the corner when it came to alcohol and drugs: it was the other temptations of life that I struggled with.

My back taxes were finally settled around this time. Megadeth made a profit from merchandise and sales of *Rust in Peace*, which came out in September 1990. It's a strange business, though. This is how the formula generally works: When gross income comes in, a manager takes 15 percent off the top, a business manager takes another 5 percent, and if the money comes in from a live concert, the agent will take another 10 percent. Out of a week's income, then, if you make $100,000—which would have been a lot of money back in those days—$30,000 would be gone off the top. So you'd be left with $70,000—but hold on. It might cost you $75,000 a week to be on tour, in which case you'd actually be losing money.

It doesn't work like that in any other business: for example, if I own a McDonald's and hire a manager, he doesn't take a percentage off the top. He is paid a salary, and if anything goes wrong, he is responsible for it and he might get fired. My dad used to say, "Your business is nothing but a bunch of con men and shysters," and the more I look at it, the more I know he was right. AC/DC said it best when they sang in "Let There Be Rock," "The guitar man got famous / The businessman got rich." It's like at casinos in Las Vegas: it's attractive for the gamblers and the tourists, but at the end of the day, all the rules favor the house.

It's the same in the music business. As attractive as it may be for a bunch of young kids to get onstage, be rock stars, and get all the chicks, drugs, and other rewards, the contracts are in favor of the record company, the concert promoter, the booking agent, and the merchandise company. These people aren't in business to lose money.

I finally figured all this out when I was clearheaded and after I'd squandered my income from our first three albums. Those years had been productive in terms of building a fan base for Megadeth, but there is a saying, "It's not how much you make, it's how much you save," and I understood that very well now. Merchandise now became crucial for paying the bills and, in my case, paying off some of my tax debt.

Our first tour of the *RiP* cycle was labeled the Clash of the Titans, with Slayer, Testament, and Suicidal Tendencies. The first leg took place in Europe in the fall of 1990. We had a long history with Slayer. We'd played together as far back as 1985, and our bands were yoked together, even though we were lyrically and thematically very different. Our fans seemed happy to coexist, and that was why we ended up doing so much stuff together over the years.

Overall, it was a good run for us, although the tides were shifting within heavy metal music. The end of hair metal was coming and the thrash metal bands were finally getting our turn at bat, which is why it was a good idea to join forces. We accomplished a lot more that way, with more money and greater opportunities. Clash of the Titans was a huge statement from our genre in these arenas. Suicidal Tendencies were popular at the time: Testament were on their way up;

and the two top bands of Megadeth and Slayer were both major forces.

We went around the world on that tour, playing with Judas Priest and Testament throughout North America in 1990 and then playing Rock in Rio in 1991. From there, we did Japan, Australia, and Hawaii. It was a great rebuilding process, and times were exciting for metal in general.

We then did a short tour of Europe in the spring of 1991, and our support group was Alice in Chains. They were a fantastic band. We'd had a lot of support acts, and a lot of them I just didn't get, but we stood by the stage and watched Alice in Chains every single night, because they were so amazingly cool.

Then we started the Clash of the Titans tour in North America with Anthrax replacing Testament, and the opening band was Alice in Chains again, whose first album, *Facelift*, had just come out. I arrived at the first show, in Dallas, and their singer Layne Staley was there. He was a very shy, soft-spoken guy offstage. He'd had his hair cut short and bleached blond, and he looked great. He told me that he'd just come out of rehab, and I said, "Rehab? For what?" He said, "Ah . . . heroin," and I said, "I just saw you a few months ago, and I never would have thought you guys did any heroin. I thought you just smoked a lot of pot."

Dave and I put our arms around him and told him that we'd been down that road and that if he needed a place of refuge out there on tour he should come to us, because we were there to help him. I think Layne stayed sober for that tour, but at some point thereafter he fell off the wagon, and I don't know if he ever got sober again before he died in 2002. It just goes to show that when you're sober, you can't ever take for granted that you'll be given that gift again. It's always easier to *stay* sober than it is to *get* sober.

It has been well documented that there was some friction between Dave and some of the other musicians on the Clash of the Titans tour, and I think I understand why. A lot of it was about jockeying for position on the tour, which was hard, because we wanted to become a united force. There were definitely some things said that made it difficult, but I played the diplomat, as usual. I handled political relations for the band and lightened the mood as necessary.

More importantly, the Clash of the Titans tour was completely sold out almost every night. It was apparent to me that this was as big as thrash metal was ever going to get, with our videos on MTV and so on. Coming off that tour, I remember sitting in the accountant's office over in West Los Angeles, and much to our surprise we had a bonus of positive cash flow from merchandise. The advances were recouped, we paid back all our debts, and I paid Dave back the remainder of a $5,000 loan he'd given me in 1989 from one of his Metallica royalty checks, when I was in financial straits from my drug use. I was on a payment plan with pretty much everybody, but I finally paid them all back. I made my last payment to the IRS and then we were finally ready to turn the page and roll into the next record, *Countdown to Extinction*. What a phenomenal way to end a year.

A THOUGHT

Letting Go Absolutely

There can be real freedom in letting go. Once we do, we are suddenly free from our past and allowed to move forward to experience life as it is meant to be, rather than how we want it to be.

Sometimes things just don't work out as we've planned, and being able to make adjustments and corrections has been key to my ability to move forward. In short, we can either be stuck in a bad situation, or we can let it go and see it as an opportunity to learn and grow.

More than anything, I've come to realize that life is a verb, not a noun. It is constantly in motion, always moving forward. The only way we can truly experience it is to be in the present, because that is where the action is. When we are stuck in our thoughts of the past (which no longer exists) or projecting images of our future (which hasn't yet happened), we rob ourselves of the here and now. And right here, right now is where life is actually going down.

CHAPTER EIGHT

The Countdown Begins

"That which doesn't kill you only makes you stronger."
—Anonymous

Our songwriting changed a bit for *Countdown to Extinction*. In 1991, we'd been playing really high-speed metal songs in big arenas like Madison Square Garden, and the sound was a little odd as a result. We started writing songs that were a little broader and more melodic. Our new mission was to create music that had more of a groove to it. Marty's writing was very melodic anyway, and the vocal lines moved in that direction, too, assisted by Max Norman, our producer. We added these great big riffs and it all came together in a perfect storm of songwriting.

We were in great spirits and the music was flowing out of us. We would go over to a rehearsal facility in Van Nuys called the Power Plant to write, shoot some hoops on our breaks, and then go in and write more songs. It was easy, it was fun, and the collective goodwill around the whole thing made it a great time. It was one of my most treasured times in all of our careers together.

By the end of 1991 Megadeth was in a great place. I was sober and more financially secure, and in Ron Laffitte we had a manager who understood heavy metal and where Megadeth fit into it. He was a fantastic manager, in a similar way that Rod Smallwood is for Iron Maiden. Some managers would have just sucked up to the singer, but that never works, and Ron didn't do that. He really grasped the bigger picture of the band working together to accomplish huge goals.

We rolled into 1992 and went into Enterprise Studios with Max Norman in Burbank and started cutting the record. Dave's son, Justis, was born at that time, so Dave had a pretty full plate of commitments between his family and the workload at the studio. Even so, the album shipped platinum. In those days you could ship a million copies and you'd get a platinum award, even if 900,000 of them were returned to the record company!

We were certified platinum in the first week. The presidents and staff at Capitol Records came down to our tour rehearsal in Santa Monica and presented us with the awards. We went around the world and did a pretty massive press junket to promote the album before it was released, and clearly those efforts paid us huge dividends upon its appearance. Dave was a correspondent for MTV, covering that year's Democratic convention, and there was a lot of mainstream press attention focused on us.

It was exciting stuff, but it was also stressful. This was a heavy workload, and rather than simply being able to sit back and enjoy the ride, we found ourselves dealing with a lot of micromanaging. We had no previous experience of celebrity on this level. It was a whole new world that we were moving through, at what felt like a really fast pace.

We did the first leg of the Countdown to Extinction tour in big arenas in Europe, and then continued in the U.S. It was very profitable. Nineteen ninety-two was the single best year of my career, financially, when I made some $500,000.

Countdown to Extinction was a major hit, debuting at Number 2 in the Billboard Top 200 in the U.S., right behind country artist Billy Ray Cyrus. We sold about 250,000 records our first week, which was huge for us, and for thrash metal in general. In December Marty and I went to Japan to set up what was essentially a sold-out tour. It was going to be huge. We got on really well and we had a great time. I remember being at a photo shoot in front of the famed Budokan and feeling that the Japanese tour in March 1993 was going to be simply fantastic.

I thought we had finally arrived. I had cleaned up my past, and the band was really firing on all cylinders. There was a general good feeling about it all. I felt as if after all these years of starvation, we'd finally begun to reap the rewards of all our hard work and discipline. We were all very excited about our futures and where we were headed. We fully expected to sell more and more records, and to get bigger and bigger.

Life, of course, has a way of deflating expectations.

We'd done a U.S. arena tour in the fall of 1992 that was very successful. However, at a show in Eugene, Oregon, on February 17, 1993, things began to shift quickly and we came off the road. It was essentially the final U.S. date for the Countdown to Extinction tour. The Japan tour was canceled, simply because the pressure of keeping Megadeth afloat at this level was causing health issues within the band.

In early 1993 Megadeth was nominated for a Grammy award, our third of the eleven nominations we've had to date. On February 24, Marty and I put our tuxedos on, rented a limo, and took our girlfriends down to the Shrine Auditorium in Los Angeles. As we were walking in, longtime supporters like Brian Slagel from Metal Blade Records were already congratulating us, saying that it was going to be a landslide and that we would easily win the Grammy. We were really excited.

We sat down and our nomination was almost immediately called, as the Best Metal Performance Grammy was one of the first to be announced. Lyle Lovett and Mary Chapin Carpenter were the presenters, and they read off the nominees for Best Metal Performance. There was a pause, during which you could hear a pin drop, and then they said, "The winner is: Nine Inch Nails."

Marty and I were completely stunned. I was in a state of shock. I was a fan of Nine Inch Nails, and I didn't know about the process of the Grammy votes, but Trent Reznor was the new kid on the block, and we had sold two million records and we were all over MTV. It seemed like that would count for something! Immediately Marty said, "I've seen enough. We're out of here." He was adamant, so we called the limo— which hadn't even found a place to park yet—and we headed up to Hollywood to grab something to eat. I don't even know how to describe that feeling. It was such a bizarre moment, because it was as if the amount of work it had taken to ramp up to that hopeful night was literally gone in a second.

Nineteen ninety-three wasn't all bad. In June we played stadium dates with Metallica, which was a great bill. Milton Keynes in England was the first one, and included Diamond Head, a favorite of both Megadeth and Metallica. The run of dates carried on into Italy, Slovenia, and Hungary. The shows were great, especially for Marty and me, who regarded Metallica as trailblazers. That band never made a wrong move. It seemed at the time that they had the Midas touch. They also have a lot of fun, and they keep things loosely tight, which I admire. There is a human quality about Metallica's songs that people ultimately relate to. I'd look at Metallica and think, "There're fifty thousand people here and they know the lyrics to every one of these songs." They were the masters of a well-run business, but they were also able to get onstage and put on a great rock 'n' roll show.

We did a big amphitheater run in the States in July '93. We were headlining, Pantera were the direct support, and White Zombie, who were an up-and-coming band, opened the show. Pantera were on the rise. I remember getting a promo copy of *Cowboys from Hell* a couple of years earlier and I could tell they were onto something big. It was the start of us going on tour with bands that went on to be much bigger than we were. In many ways, Pantera screamed right past us after their next album, owing in large part to some of our own internal issues and tours that were canceled or postponed on the Countdown tour cycle.

Rex Brown (Pantera, Kill Devil Hill): David Ellefson has been the epitome of the solid metal bassist as long as I've known him. His style is impeccable. He's also a great ambassador for sharing his style with so many, with his unique clinics.

That particular amphitheater run was mapped out to be a six-week tour for us, and it would have been very advantageous for all three bands in our careers. It would have been a nice financial windfall for all of us as well. Sadly, the tour was shortened and we instead booked dates with Aerosmith. Unfortunately, that tour also came to a sudden and unexpected end. As I see it, the worst possible way to make a business decision is to base it on sobriety, which was part of our motive to tour with Aerosmith. Business decisions need to be based on business—period. Both Aerosmith and Megadeth were at the peak of their careers at the time, but the two bands were clearly not a good match.

I remember the Aerosmith tour started in Mobile, Alabama, and then we went to Little Rock, Arkansas. At the second show, Steven Tyler came into our dressing room as he had heard that Dave was upset about production issues on the tour. We weren't getting a sound check or much space onstage, and we couldn't have a backdrop. I agreed with Dave on this. We weren't a baby band of the kind that Aerosmith often took out on tour with them as their openers. We had paid our dues, and we didn't deserve to be treated like the new kids on the block. As long as we were onstage, we wanted it to be a Megadeth show, but it clearly wasn't that.

Steven came into our dressing room to talk with Dave and I remember him being very cool. He said, "I hear there are some problems. Is there anything I can do?" I thought that was very considerate of him, since he certainly didn't have to do that, as the CEO of Aerosmith. He explained to Dave that he had walked similar roads and that if Dave ever needed him, he'd be there.

I took the opportunity to bring up Steven's sobriety phone call to me years earlier. I said to him, "You probably won't remember this, but about six years ago you actually called to talk sobriety with me when I was in my addiction," and I thanked him for that.

That moment passed, though—and a couple of shows later we were fired off the Aerosmith tour. We had driven to Lubbock, Texas, where we were going to play the Civic Center. We were staying at the Holiday Inn, just a couple of blocks down from the arena. Nick, Marty, and I got off the bus and walked across the street to this little Mexican restaurant. The waitress asked, "What y'all doing in town?" and we told her that we were in Megadeth. She said "Megadeth? What are you doing here? We heard Jackyl was going to be at the show tonight. I heard it on the radio!" So we went to the pay phone—cell phones weren't quite commonplace yet—called our tour manager and asked, "What's the deal?" He said, "I know, I know. . . . I'm booking flights home right now." Our hearts sank. How ironic that the hostess at the Mexican restaurant knew about us being fired off the tour before we did.

I remember flying home that night and feeling like I'd been kicked in the gut for the third time on this Countdown tour. Japan had been canceled, not once but twice; we'd let go of the six-week tour with Pantera and White Zombie; and now we were getting fired off the Aerosmith tour. It was like three shots to the head. We were so deflated. It was the beginning of the end for Marty: it really took the wind out of his sails.

But we had to move forward. A new album, which we planned to call *Youthanasia*, was scheduled for release in 1994, and we regrouped to write it. During that process, two life-changing events took place for me, and what is more, they occurred on the very same day.

I'd known my girlfriend Julie Foley since 1988, when she worked for Doug Thaler, one of the partners at McGhee Entertainment. McGhee had some of the biggest names in rock 'n' roll such as Bon Jovi, Mötley Crüe, the Scorpions, and Skid Row. It seemed like a really good opportunity for us to sign up with their firm. Julie and I really fell for each other, which was a little weird because we worked together. Dating the girl at the office is generally a business no-no. Yet at the same time, there was something there between us.

I remember our first date. Julie took me to a Los Angeles Kings hockey game as their office always had season seats to the hip sports events in town. To start, we went to a Mexican restaurant on Sunset Boulevard, and from there I had to make a stop at a drug dealer to pick up some cocaine before we went to the game, which I think she thought was a little odd. She eventually asked me some years back why I didn't drink on that first date, and I told her it was because I was on heroin. When McGhee Entertainment dropped Megadeth, partly because I failed to complete rehab, Julie and I said good-bye. I thought that was the end of it. But when I sobered up in 1990, I gave Julie a call, and we became friends. We then began to date and fell for each other again. It truly was a new beginning for us.

Julie has put up with a lot from me over the years. The unspoken attitude of rock 'n' roll is "I get to do whatever I want. Don't you all wish you were me?" With all of the best rock 'n' rollers, whether it be David Lee Roth or Jim Morrison, the message is that we get to live a life where you don't have to go to work, you can drink and do drugs and be with chicks all day. However, being sober, I'm called to a new standard. If you take away the sex and the drugs, you're left with the rock 'n' roll, which was an awakening for me because it brought me back to why I got into music in the first place when I was eleven years old. It was purely for the love of rock 'n' roll. How ironic that I'd come full circle.

That's really been my journey up to the present day, and sobriety has allowed me to have a daily diligence and to be aware of the distractions. Drugs, women, envy of other people, pride, gluttony, worrying that if one band sells a million albums, then we need to sell two million—these are human fears and temptations and they exist for all of us, but they are magnified in this particular industry. Addictions can magnify them even more.

In late 1993 Julie quit her job with Doug Thaler, who had moved on from McGhee Entertainment to start his own company, Top Rock Development Corporation. Julie was his top employee and office manager, and Mötley Crüe was their number-one act. This was around the time that Mötley parted ways with their singer Vince Neil. Julie felt that it was time to move on, and that her time was done at that company. She had no regrets, as she had enjoyed a really exciting and fun career in artist management.

Now that I wasn't using drugs or drinking, I had some reserves of money saved up. Julie had been flying out to Scottsdale, Arizona, every weekend and looking at homes, as we were ready for a new adventure outside the hustle and bustle of Los Angeles. Plus, as a musician in a global band, I didn't have to live in the city any longer, as I did when I started my career there in 1983. So we moved to Scottsdale in September 1993 and bought our first house.

It was a leap of faith to move out to Arizona and leave the music hub of Los Angeles. Add to that the financial responsibilities of buying a home and cars and developing a life together as a family, especially with the volatility that comes with life in a rock band. Dave and his family had also moved out to Arizona a couple months prior, so it was just the two of us band members making the migration at that point. I only knew one other person in town. His name was Craig S., and he was a real guru in the Phoenix recovery community.

Beyond our buying a home, the move to Scottsdale was really a major life changer for me and Julie. That was when I joined the recovery program for real as an active member, not just to show up late at the meetings and sit at the back as I so often did in L.A. I found it difficult to develop strong ties with the recovery community in Los Angeles in my early sobriety, but in Phoenix it was easier and much more relaxed. I learned to arrive early and be an active participant in the program. Craig became my official new sponsor, and I really went through the process top to bottom. I realized that I was capable of a lot of destruction, even as a sober guy. In order to keep that tendency in check I rigorously practiced the principles of recovery.

After the songwriting for the *Youthanasia* record in early 1994, there was a two-week break. Julie and I flew to Hawaii for a quick vacation getaway. It was on that vacation that I proposed marriage to her. I was lying on a massage couch one morning at the hotel, and midmassage it just hit me that I should marry her on this trip. Originally, this had been just a vacation, nothing more. However, it was such an amazingly powerful inspiration that came over me. I went upstairs to our hotel room and proposed to her, right then and there. I said to her, "Why don't we just get married while we're out here, rather than having to plan for a big wedding and reception? Plus, we can hold a celebration when we get home to Arizona for all of our friends and family." She accepted and agreed, and we bought a ring later that day. We found a pastor and we arranged to get married on the beach of Wailea, Maui, on April 2, two days later.

Before the ceremony on the morning of April 2, Julie and I went down to the restaurant to have breakfast. Afterward we went up to our hotel room, and I saw that the red message light was blinking on the telephone by the bed. I called voice mail and there was a message from our next-door neighbor back home in Scottsdale. Her name was Lori and she had been watching our house while we were away. She was crying on the message, and she said, "David, something terrible has happened to your dad. You need to call home immediately." My heart sank. I knew my dad had been admitted to the Mayo Clinic in Rochester, Minnesota, the week of our trip, because he had ongoing heart problems.

I immediately called my brother and my mom back home, and it turned out that my dad had passed away the previous night from congestive heart failure. He was sixty-nine. I was stunned. It was bittersweet, to say the very least, to get married on the same day that I lost my father. I was sobbing all the way through the wedding ceremony on the back lawn of the hotel, by the beach. One Ellefson had passed, yet another came into the family, on the very same day.

We cut the honeymoon short and flew back to Minnesota for my dad's funeral two days later. My mom told me that my father had said to her, "I hope David and Julie take care of each other out in Hawaii." He wanted me to marry her, and here I was returning to Minnesota with Julie as my wife—to attend his funeral.

By April 1994, my old life had been washed away.

A THOUGHT
Marriage

Getting married was one of the most trusting processes in the world for me, because it truly meant letting go of my past. It also meant partnership with another person on a whole new level. Julie wasn't a groupie rock 'n' roll girl. She was the real deal, with a good head on her shoulders, and she has become the true champion of our household in the years after we married, especially raising our two children.

What's even more humbling is that we often mirror the examples set before us by our parents. I was lucky that my parents were married until the day my father passed away. They set a good example for me in marriage, as did Julie's parents. My father was a real straight shooter, and knowing that our marriage was finally in place was one of the best gifts I could have given him at the end of his life.

Jackson
Minnesota

My hometown of Jackson, Minnesota, pictured here in the 1960s when I was a young kid. Our family farm was six miles to the north. It is a wholesome, friendly town of about 3,500 people, initially built on the Des Moines River to support the local farming community as far back as the 1800s.

My mother's parents, Isabel and Arthur Jorgenson, on their farm in Gillett Grove, Iowa, where I spent many summers shooting guns and learning about model railroads.

My father, Gordon Ellefson, in his younger days. He was a conservative man who believed in hard work and discipline, but who also supported me fully with my dreams of becoming a professional musician. I am grateful to him to this day.

My paternal grandparents, Henry and Anna Ellefson, pictured holding me as a baby in late November 1964.

My brother, Eliot, and me as toddlers.

The farm where I grew up in Jackson, Minnesota. On the far right you can see the white work sheds where I spent my teenage years rehearsing with my bands Toz and Killers. Quite a different backdrop from the jungles of Los Angeles.

A photo of me in kindergarten.
Even a state-of-the-art, heavy metal titan
has to start somewhere, right?

Eliot and me in 1969 next to one of our John Deere tractors on the farm. This
picture illustrates the harsh winters we endured out in rural Minnesota.

Here we are again in
1969 on the farm, with
at least six feet of snow
to contend with. No
wonder I wanted to
move to California!

A picture of me in first grade. I was shy and reserved, but my life would soon change when I got my first bass guitar a few years later.

My family in the early 1970s. We were a close unit, although my future was never going to be in farming.

8. Someday, I am going to - be a famous rock musician.

9. When I get out of school, I am going to - go to a large town, + get a good band together, + put out all of my effort into a rock band.

10. My biggest problem right now is - nothing.

11. The most important thing to me right now is - friends, girls, family + music.

12. For a lifetime occupation, I would like to - be a serious musician.

Some of my ninth-grade goals and achievements from high school health class. Notice that rock music was all-encompassing to me. I also notice some of my better character traits developing here, too.

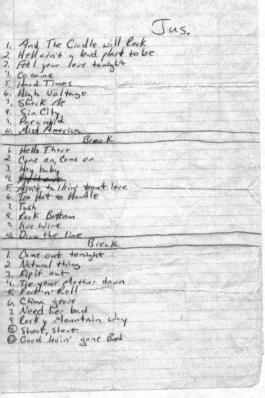

Jus.

1. And The Cradle will Rock
2. Hell ain't a bad place to be
3. Feel your love tonight
4. Cocaine
5. Hard Times
6. High Voltage
7. Shock Me
8. Sin City
9. Paranoid
10. Miss America

Break

1. Hello There
2. Come on, Come on
3. Hey baby
4. Riff Raff
5. Ain't talking 'bout love
6. Too Hot to Handle
7. Tush
8. Rock Bottom
9. Live Wire
10. Draw the line

Break

1. Come out tonight
2. Natural thing
3. Rip it out
4. Tie your Mother down
5. Rock'n'Roll
6. China grove
7. Need her bad
8. Rocky Mountain Way
9. Shoot, shoot
10. Good lovin' gone Bad

A Toz set list. Classic tunes, every one!

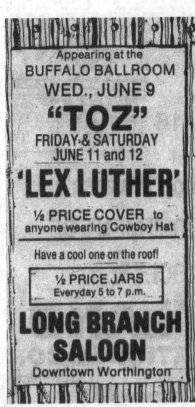

A Toz show ad in one of our local newspapers from the early 1980s. Notice the "half price cover charge to anyone wearing a cowboy hat." The things you have to do to pull in a crowd!

KILLERS

A promo photo for my band Killers, which was Toz's new name. We chose it in homage to the second LP from Iron Maiden, whose music had become a profound influence on us. I've been in bands since I was twelve years old, and it doesn't look like I'll be stopping anytime soon. Man, we looked scary!

In 1983, I was interviewed for this career-planning program. I wasn't a bad student, but I had no interest whatsoever in pursuing further education or a career outside rock music. I was totally single-minded in my obsession with music during my teenage years.

My high school senior year report card. Note the sarcastic comment from one of the teachers, wishing me the best of luck with my music career.

My high school graduation photo: I was young and full of optimism.

Jump forward to 1986; Dave and I went back to visit the farm after Megadeth finished recording *Peace Sells . . . but Who's Buying?* From left: Brad Schmidt, who moved to California with me in 1983; me; Dave Mustaine; Greg Handevidt; and Toz roadie Jeff Yonker.

Me and my best buddy Greg Handevidt in the basement of the family farmhouse in 1986. We'd been through a lot together in our early bands Toz and Killers, as well as during our move to California in 1983. We've remained best friends to this day.

Me with my parents on the Megadeth tour bus in 1988 during *the So Far, So Good . . . So What!* European tour.

Here I am with my mother in Paris during 1988. My parents made the trip over to Europe to see me while I was on tour.

Safely back home in Minnesota with my family in 1989. Note the Megadeth gold disc on the wall. Despite the long, hard road of rock 'n' roll, I was starting to achieve my musical goals.

Our wedding reception at the Scottsdale Princess resort in Scottsdale, Arizona, in June 1994. Dave Mustaine offers a wedding toast to Julie and me, while our producer Max Norman watches in the background.

With Julie's family at our wedding reception.

Me and Julie outside our first home, which we purchased in Scottsdale, Arizona, in 1993.

Onstage with the late, great Ronnie Montrose circa 2006. With Montrose I was able to really branch out to explore new styles of expression on the bass guitar. (Picture courtesy of Robert Tuozzo)

I'm pictured here with the late Craig S., my sponsor for many years in Phoenix. He was a wise man from whom I learned much about recovery from addiction. I probably wouldn't be here today without him. R.I.P.

F5, pictured at the Dallas Guitar Show in 2006. From left: John Davis, me, Dale Steele, Steve Conley, Dave Small. (Picture courtesy of Fran Strine)

Elliot Easton of the Cars, producer Mark Hudson, and me at the Rock and Roll Fantasy Camp Hawaii in 2008. I was a huge fan of Elliot's guitar work, and Mark really taught me the value of knowing all the great classic rock songs.

Me and Julie, pictured at Shepherd of the Desert Lutheran Church and School, where we started MEGA Life! in 2006.

A couple of Julie's greatest strengths are hospitality and mothering. Here she is volunteering at lunch at the kids' school.

Me as Cub Scout leader for my son, Roman, and his den of scouts. The school principal nominated me as leader, so I accepted the challenge. These are the kinds of things that brought about new meaning in my life as a young father.

Here I am as the T-ball assistant coach for my daughter, Athena, in 2008. Over the years, sports became a huge part of our family's bonding time together.

Me and Roman at a New Jersey beach on a day off from tour. Note his classic T-shirt: like father, like son!

Heavy metal supergroup Hail! pictured at a mosque in Istanbul in 2009. From left: Tim "Ripper" Owens, me, Andreas Kisser, and Jimmy DeGrasso.

Julie and me outside our home in Scottsdale in 2009.

My first cover in *Bass Player* magazine, in 2010, with my treasured signature Jackson bass. This was one of many great milestones in my career to date.

My dad's sister, Mary Ann Werner, with my kids, Roman and Athena. Mary Ann is the last surviving member of that generation of Ellefsons. She and my father used to be in the farming business together. She still makes the best banana bread around!

The Ellefson family on a visit to Minnesota in 2012.

Me, Eliot, my mom, and our families back on the farm in Minnesota.

MODERN PLAYER TELECASTER BASS TESTED

THE UK'S NUMBER ONE BASS GUITAR MAGAZINE

Bass

r Magazine

SIVE
**AVID
LLEFSON**
GADETH REUNION AND
SIGNATURE BASS

**ARK
OPPUS**
NK 182
D BETTER
ER!

VED
JE
VATT-ROY

N TO PLAY
VICTOR WOOTEN
mb Slap Techniques Explained

OVERWATER
INSPIRATION 5 AND
ASPIRATION ELITE 4
Top Quality For All!

FEATURE
**NAMM 2012
SHOW REPORT**
We Bring You The Hottest
Bass Products

TESTED
**EBS
REIDMAR 250**
Light And Compact With Huge Tones

www.bassguitarmagazine.com

The cover of *Bass Guitar Magazine* (UK) in 2012. Who'd have thought the kid from the farm in Minnesota would ever make it this far?

Athena and me pictured outside the Grammy Awards ceremony in 2013. I was so proud to let my daughter experience something so monumental with me.

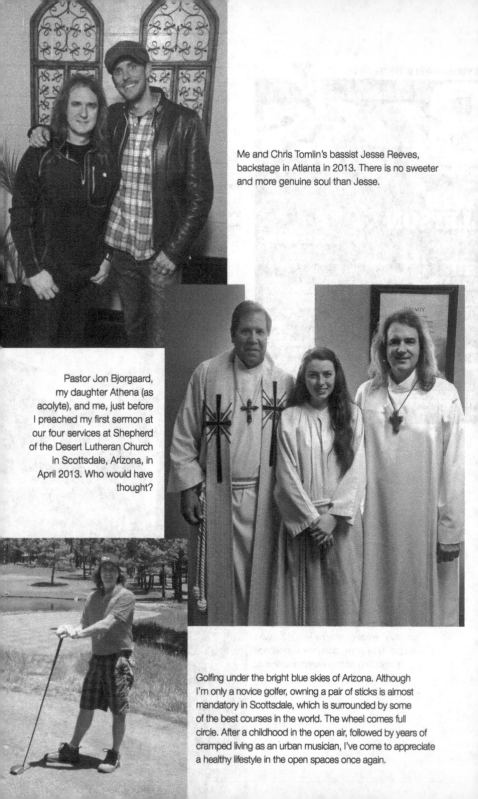

Me and Chris Tomlin's bassist Jesse Reeves, backstage in Atlanta in 2013. There is no sweeter and more genuine soul than Jesse.

Pastor Jon Bjorgaard, my daughter Athena (as acolyte), and me, just before I preached my first sermon at our four services at Shepherd of the Desert Lutheran Church in Scottsdale, Arizona, in April 2013. Who would have thought?

Golfing under the bright blue skies of Arizona. Although I'm only a novice golfer, owning a pair of sticks is almost mandatory in Scottsdale, which is surrounded by some of the best courses in the world. The wheel comes full circle. After a childhood in the open air, followed by years of cramped living as an urban musician, I've come to appreciate a healthy lifestyle in the open spaces once again.

CHAPTER NINE

The End of an Era

"Most people adjust their lives to meet their goals, but
addicts adjust their goals to meet their lives."

—Anonymous

Life goes on despite the sadness of bereavement, and I remained on pretty solid ground with my new life during this period. There really is strength in numbers when you're trying to move away from old playgrounds, playmates, and playthings. This was the first big proving ground for me of my motivation for being clean. When I watched other addicts go back down the old roads, it initially looked like fun. It was the morning after that didn't look so pretty.

Megadeth continued to work as prolifically as ever. In 1993, we recorded a song for the Beavis and Butt-Head compilation album *The Beavis and Butt-Head Experience*. At the same time, we were also asked to cover a Black Sabbath song for the *Nativity in Black* tribute album. We went into that session at Enterprise Studios in Burbank, where we had done *Countdown to Extinction*, and right away I suggested that we do "Paranoid." It was easy, and it was one of the more popular Sabbath songs. I used to play it in cover bands back in Minnesota. It was a no-brainer.

When Dave called, saying he wanted to get started on our next album, *Youthanasia*, it was a real relief for me to start working again. From a recovery point of view I had never sat down and made amends with him before. In early 1994 I sat down with him at the Orange Tree resort in Phoenix, where he and I sometimes played golf together, and I made amends with him. It was important that I clear my side of the street, and I felt it necessary to sit down man-to-man and clean a few things up. You can't walk around with a life of resentment. It was great, because it started a new journey for us.

This was an exciting time, personally as well as professionally. When we moved out to Arizona, Julie cashed in her pension and put it in the bank. I had bought our house, but it was a little scary because I had taken this risk assuming that we would record another Megadeth album. It was a real leap of faith, and I had no backup plan. After all, I had no plans for a solo career. I grew up wanting to be in a band, because I was seeking camaraderie and a brotherhood to lock arms with. I wanted the band to work.

I started writing some songs with a friend of mine, Pat Schunk, who was a great guy from the Midwest I'd met through Nick Menza. Nick, Pat, and I would go mountain biking in the hills of Los Angeles just above the San Fernando Valley, in and around the *Rust in Peace* and *Countdown to Extinction* records. We hit it off and started writing some tunes together at his home in Studio City, a few blocks from where I lived at the time.

After we compiled a dozen songs or so I started shopping some of them around to friends at record labels and other music publishers. Megadeth was big enough that when I rang people in the industry, they would take my call. I realized that if my time in Megadeth ever came to an end, I might be able to continue a career in rock music. You don't just become a solo artist, but I did enjoy the songwriting process and registered the songs with EMI Music Publishing. I even submitted a few of them to Megadeth to consider for *Youthanasia*, but I soon realized that they weren't written in the same spirit. They weren't heavy metal songs.

It was good to get involved in the songwriting process with people outside the band. It not only gave me a greater appreciation for Megadeth, but it opened me up musically. I revisited instruments I would never be able to play in the band, such as keyboards and acoustic guitar. I learned to appreciate the skill of writing other kinds of music. Moreover, I got to experience some real producing, even if it was just for myself. Understanding the layering of instruments and working with other professional players is a process I still enjoy. A highlight of those sessions was when I hired John Bush of Armored Saint and Anthrax to sing on one of the songs. Those songs are still there, and effectively make up a solo album if I ever choose to make one.

The initial idea for *Youthanasia* was to rent a big house out in Arizona, where Dave and I now lived, and move a studio into it and make a record there. The producer Max Norman flew out, but we couldn't find the right house where we could effectively carry out our endeavor. We started looking at some commercial spaces and found a 10,000-square-foot place just southwest of downtown Phoenix. Definitely not a great neighborhood, but the building was perfect.

We leased the place for six months. Max built three isolation rooms for recording in the building, which he would later dismantle and take back to L.A. to build his own studio. Mick Zane of the band Malice was Max's buddy, and had a day job building sets at one of the Hollywood film studios. He became one of the chief carpenters on the project to help Max build the studio. It was incredible that Max not only oversaw the record production but also designed and built a studio in Arizona, all the while tending to his family back in Los Angeles. Truly a man of many talents and much energy.

At the same time, we were rehearsing at Phase Four Studios down in Tempe, where we spent five days a week running through song ideas and getting them together. We had realized that a lot of music you hear on the radio is at 120 beats per minute, because that's around the same pace as an active human heart rate. We talked to Max about the tempos and also the tunings, in order to refine the songwriting. We went to another studio in central Phoenix called Vintage Recorders, where we did the final writing.

Since *Rust in Peace*, we'd had a sort of spiritual sobriety guru around us, to help us work through our issues as they arose. Having a counselor available to help us communicate and resolve things was quite effective. Most big companies have a human resources department; most rock bands don't. Counselors fulfilled that role for us. Friends and fans would sometimes remark about the same matters in the Metallica movie *Some Kind of Monster*, to which I would reply, "Yep, been there, done that!" Honestly, I understood it, because we'd been through something similar, which had been helpful in the rebuilding process around *Rust in Peace*.

In Phoenix we were introduced to a business development coach named Daniel. One of his main areas of focus was team building. Businesses hire these people to analyze their structure, spot weaknesses, and help fix them. There was almost a corporate mind-set about Megadeth at this time. It was quite a contrast to be asking how we could create and control our business in the middle of all our creativity, though. Somehow we made it work, as we were heading into uncharted waters with our success.

We rolled into *Youthanasia* with a lot of optimism, and the first single, "Train of Consequences," was greeted with a lot of fanfare in the press. MTV had us come out and play a Halloween show called Night of the Living Megadeth in New York City. During the set, Dave made a comment when introducing a brand-new track called "A Tout le Monde" along the lines of "This is a song about how I tried to kill myself." He was actually referring to another one of our songs, "Skin o' My Teeth." Regardless, "A Tout le Monde" was scheduled as our next single, and we'd spent a lot of money shooting a video for it with

Wayne Isham, who had done the video for "Train of Consequences" and other videos from *Countdown to Extinction*. When we submitted the video to MTV, they rejected it. We were shocked and asked them why. They told us that they didn't like the lyrical content, so we reedited it for them, but it was dead in the water. It was a real blow to our campaign in the U.S.

Adding to this mishap, times were changing musically, too. *Youthanasia* was popular internationally, but sold only half as much in the United States as *Countdown to Extinction*, though not because of its merits as a record. The bigger issue was that, in 1994, the Seattle bands were coming to the fore. The only real metal band to survive that change was Metallica, but even they cut their hair and changed their look and their sound. They were still very popular, though, and when you're that high up, any glide downward takes a very long time.

For the most part, thrash metal fell from its throne, and Megadeth spent the rest of the 1990s, with *Cryptic Writings* and *Risk*, trying to navigate a very challenging music business. We had to think like businessmen—almost like marketing executives—rather than simply musicians with guitars around our necks. This was the reality of us simply wanting to continue to be Megadeth, unlike so many of our contemporaries who just got swept away by the winds of change.

All of a sudden, MTV was very clearly not playing heavy metal videos. It was all Seattle and grunge bands like Pearl Jam, Nirvana, and Alice in Chains. By the time we released *Cryptic Writings* in 1997, we had realized that mainstream music channels were simply not going to play our videos any more. Fortunately, MTV didn't make Megadeth, and we had a fan base that we knew was going to be there even when our videos weren't being played. That is the power of heavy metal and our fans. Nonetheless, MTV had taken us from being a band that played 500-seat clubs to arenas through sheer exposure, so we certainly weren't unappreciative, either.

I remember when our booking agent flew out to present us with the schedule for the Youthanasia tour: it was a list of midsize halls. Although it would have been wise to start small and build up, we wanted to keep the profile of the band large and still play arenas. We went out with four trucks and three buses to commence the U.S. tour. This wasn't a fatal move by any means, but we ended up coming home and having to readjust our game plan. We had to, if we wanted to survive the music business changes, especially those that affected heavy metal. We always liked to quote Clint Eastwood in the movie *Heartbreak Ridge* when he said that sometimes one has to "overcome, adapt, and improvise." That became us.

As we went around the world promoting the new record, I had the idea of writing a book. I'd been writing a few columns for magazines, and I'd been reading a lot of self-help and motivational books, and although that wasn't my area of expertise I certainly knew a lot about the music business. Although you can go to college and learn how to play your instrument, there's nowhere you can go to actually learn about the industry—at least, there wasn't in those days. For the most part we were all just winging it and learning the business on the fly.

So I wrote this book, which was published in 1997, called *Making Music Your Business: A Guide for Young Musicians*. At the same time *Bass Player* magazine, whose publisher later issued my book, asked me to become a regular monthly columnist. This process started around the time of *Youthanasia* and gave me an interesting creative outlet as I traveled around the world during that twelve-month tour cycle.

By the end of 1995, our manager Ron Laffitte was getting disheartened. We'd been through the *Countdown to Extinction* years of popularity, with all those huge highs and lows, and with all of the music industry changes I often couldn't help but feel as if our ship had sailed. It felt as if there were so many things in our lives that were out of our control. It was a sad reality that we never discussed, but that we all recognized.

Ron accepted a position in charge of the West Coast division of Elektra Records, and although his plan was to manage Megadeth and work for Elektra, I could tell that Ron—who had pulled us out of the scrap heap back in 1989 with *Rust in Peace*, only to see us get knocked back over and over again in ensuing years—was getting burned out.

For whatever reason, there's a two-album cycle for most people around Megadeth, whether they're producers, managers, agents, or road personnel, and Ron had survived three. Ron had initially brought us to a meeting with Iron Maiden's manager Rod Smallwood back in 1987 or '88, but Rod was not that interested in us at that time because we were pretty unstable and all of his bands were successful. However, in 1995 Dave and I took another meeting with Rod over dinner in Paris, with the idea that he would begin to manage us. His view was that we should make another album and come back to play in Europe, and then tour and tour and tour. Dave and I felt that while this would be great for our overseas audiences, we had sold millions of records in the U.S., and we'd be risking our appeal back home, which was still our primary market.

We did one final U.S. tour in 1995. Our support act on the tour was Corrosion of Conformity. Dave struck up a correspondence with their manager Mike Renault, a former soundman for Journey back in their glory days. One thing I've always found about managers who have come from the road is that they're all about the nuts and bolts, and they really service the mechanics of a rock band on the road very well. They understand the fundamentals and, most important, they understand how to balance a budget.

A lot of guys in the music business have a top-down approach up in the stratosphere, and they like to drive fancy cars and live in nice houses, but they don't like to get their hands dirty. The guys who come up from the bottom are the opposite of that, so we hired Mike and his senior partner Bud Prager. I was a little unsure about this. Mike was very pragmatic but Bud was an older, white-haired gentleman and he didn't seem to have much interest in us, probably just because of his age. Anyway, we hired them as managers by early 1996.

We felt a new, but more realistic, optimism on the next cycle as we went into Vintage Recorders studio in central Phoenix to begin the songwriting for our next record, *Cryptic Writings*. My son, Roman, had been born on February 2, 1996, and the sleep deprivation for Julie and me was a nightmare. I'd never experienced anything like it. Thankfully, the songwriting sessions became a sort of mandatory schedule to settle our home life a bit, as we determined 10 A.M. as the start time for the sessions. This meant we had to get some sleep in order for me to not feel deliriously like killing everyone each day from the lack of rest.

During the writing at Vintage studios, I would hit noon sobriety meetings a few blocks away, where my sponsor Craig S. oversaw a half-way house for newly sober clients. This gave me a priority for sobriety and some time away from our guitars. Incidentally, that halfway house inspired Dave to write the song "Use the Man" on the upcoming album, based on an incident at the time where a client relapsed and was found dead with a needle in his arm. The morbid, sad reality of addiction remained with us, despite the sobriety around us.

We ended up with eighteen new original songs, and headed to Nashville in September 1996 to begin the recording of *Cryptic Writings* with producer Dann Huff, whose work with the rock band Giant had impressed us. Our new management team of Mike Renault and Bud Prager helped us team up with Dann, as Bud had managed Giant in years past. Dann had been a major player in the Los Angeles session scene back in the 1980s and early '90s and had relocated to Nashville at the forefront of the new-country movement, which included super-stars like Garth Brooks, Shania Twain, and Alan Jackson. That movement welcomed the L.A. session players with open arms, as guys like Dann were real guitar shredders. They brought with them a modern rock and pop edge that ultimately changed Nashville and the sound of country music.

Dann had just launched his producing career with a country group called Lonestar. *Cryptic Writings* was his second production job, and it was a good pairing because we were all great musicians. Personally, I was a little nervous about the session due to the heavyweight roster and caliber of bassists in Nashville, so I took some bass lessons in

Phoenix in mid-1996 with my friend Ray Riendeau, who later became the bassist in Halford.

When we arrived in Nashville, we set up several days of preproduction at a large rehearsal complex called Soundcheck on the east side of town. All the major artists rehearsed there, although it turned out we were the first major metal band to ever record in the town. With Dann, a true renegade in his own right, we brought a lot of attention to the session, and to this day Megadeth enjoys a certain level of musical respect in Nashville.

Soundcheck was also home to many artist-relations offices for the major musical equipment manufacturers. This led me to an introduction to Peavey Electronics. Unhappy with my Ampeg SVT rig for the band's sound at that time, I wheeled in two Peavey 810 TVX cabinets and their KiloBass 1,000-watt digital bass head, which blew all of my gear out of the water. Even with the volume set low, Dave and Marty would continually ask me to turn down the volume. I was in heaven. After all those years I had finally discovered an amp that was actually louder than the roar of the Marshall guitar stacks I was always competing with. To this day, the bass tone on *Cryptic Writings* is my benchmark favorite of everything I've ever recorded.

I stayed in Nashville for three weeks, rehearsing and recording my bass parts for the album. It wasn't all fun: the pillows at the hotel where we stayed gave me a terrible kink in my neck and I was missing my six-month-old son, Roman, more than I had ever missed anyone in my life. It was killing me to be away from him. I realized that the love you feel for your children can never be equaled by love for anything, or anyone.

When I got back to Phoenix in October, Julie and Roman met me at the airport. As I was putting my bags into the back of our Jeep, Roman suddenly looked up at me, as if to say, "It's that guy again!" I picked him up out of his stroller and he clung to me like a little koala bear. That began a father-and-son relationship like no other. He cried incessantly when I left for tours, crawling and walking around the house looking for me. I don't know which of us missed the other more.

A few months later Dave came to my house to play me the mixed and mastered version of the album. I was blown away. For the first time ever, our records had a seasoned professional sound that made them come off like star records, not just recordings of our songs. There was magic in the mix, and we sounded much better than I remembered when the songs were being recorded. That gave us something to shoot for in the quality of the live shows that followed.

The album cycle started with an undercover warm-up show at the Electric Ballroom in Phoenix, under the pseudonym Vic & the Rattleheads. This was followed by a national radio broadcast by Westwood One, recorded live the next night from the Mesa Amphitheatre in Mesa, Arizona, to a sold-out crowd. By this time, the lead single, "Trust," was a number-one smash hit on the U.S.'s Active Rock radio format.

We had now successfully transformed ourselves from being merely a thrash metal band into the mainstream. Although *Youthanasia* was a pivotal point, *Cryptic Writings* was the real deal. This whole period was a real leap forward for the band. We'd fought hard for success, and we got it.

This time was also one of great change for me personally, in terms of my development as a human being. New priorities fell into place for me around *Cryptic Writings*. Back in 1983 when I first moved to California, my focus was solely work, work, work: Megadeth, Megadeth, Megadeth. That's why if you're going to start a rock band, you should do it when you're eighteen years old. You may as well get in the game as early as you can, because at that age you don't have other responsibilities.

Cryptic Writings gave us three more top-five Active Rock hits in the U.S. These effectively reinvented the band in the U.S. mainstream and propelled us on an eighteen-month world tour. We toured several times around the country, flew twice to Europe and Japan, and then headed to South America. The songs were heavy but hooky, and, just like with *Countdown to Extinction*, we were in favor in the mainstream.

This time, of course, we had done it without TV exposure, as that had completely dried up, at least domestically.

Because of our radio success, Dave was often asked to go on early-morning radio shows and play golf with radio station bigwigs and program directors—people who could make you or crush you in a single blow during their weekly programming meetings. He was great at the politics of that game and really helped push the wind into our sails on radio because of those efforts. Capitol Records was spending huge money on our radio campaign and it was working.

If you think you end up on radio just because you wrote a good song, guess again—it's pay to play, or at least it was back then. This period marked the end of that form of radio corruption. Fortunately, we got to enjoy the ride before it all ended up in court between the radio industry and the U.S. justice system, only a few years later.

Turbulence was coming, however, and it was soon Nick Menza's turn to leave the band. He was replaced by Jimmy DeGrasso only ten days before we commenced the Ozzfest tour of the U.S. in the summer of 1998. I was sad, because I had supported Nick for all those years, but when his playing began to hurt the band's live performances I gave Dave my blessing to stop fighting him on it and the change was made. Jimmy's audition was in front of five thousand people at a sold-out show in Fresno. He played flawlessly, which was a real eye-opener for me. Once more, the caliber of the players in this business was proven to me. For him to play eighteen songs that well, with no rehearsal, was amazing. I took that lesson seriously—and it was very useful to me in later years.

Jimmy's excellent sense of timing revealed that Dave, Marty, and I had developed some bad habits together in the former lineup, a common tendency when musicians play together for a long time. Jimmy's playing brought these issues immediately to light. However, those habits were part of the charm of the *Rust in Peace* lineup, and our fans liked them. Our timing might not have been perfect, but we executed the music with ferocity. That vibe and punch could never be duplicated with any other lineup, and the fans knew it. Another lesson: sometimes it's not about being perfect, it's about having vibe.

We carved out most of October for me to be home for her birth. Megadeth was in South America in the earlier part of that month, and when I called home Julie would tell me of small pains that might signal the onset of the birth. I begged her to keep her legs crossed until I got home, so I could be there to greet Athena. Athena Grace Ellefson was born a couple weeks later on October 23, 1998, in Scottsdale, so I was able to be there for her birth.

After a final trip to Japan a few weeks later in November, we headed home. The tour ended on a high note with much success, many accolades, and plenty of money to divide up from our merchandise take. Could we sustain this level of success? Well, let's look at it like this. When we released our next album a year later, it appeared at the same time as enormously successful albums by new bands such as Godsmack, Slipknot, Limp Bizkit, and Disturbed. I think that explains everything about where we were in the scheme of things and the wisdom of those who were guiding us into the next album.

A THOUGHT
Parenthood

One of the first things any seasoned parent will tell you is how much your life will change when you have kids. Intellectually it makes sense, but you don't really grasp it until the day it happens.

All those parents before us were right: kids do change everything, especially your priorities. For me, fatherhood has been about rearranging my priorities in all that I think, say, and do. This includes faith, money, and career decisions and everything else, too. In fact, the measure of being a good father isn't so much what we do but rather how we *prioritize* what we do.

To this day, I think every opportunity that comes my way is always followed by the immediate thought of "How will this affect my family?" Even touring raises those questions. Julie constantly reminds me of how blessed I am to be able to go out and do what I love for a living by playing music. That's why, once I come home off the road, I usually get about one day's grace to be the hero for the day with the family. The next day, it's off to the back of the line, and time to roll up my sleeves and be Dad again.

That's probably the most difficult part of being a touring rock musician—the constant ego check that comes from your family. It's great to have everyone give you attention, but when you face the reality of having kids, they are the ones who really need attention—because kids don't raise themselves.

Parenthood has been a tremendous blessing: it makes me check my ego at the door and think of someone else's needs beside my own.

CHAPTER TEN

Absolute Power Corrupts Absolutely

> "'For I know the plans I have for you,' says the Lord. 'Plans to prosper you and not to harm you, plans to give you hope and a future.'"
>
> —Jeremiah 29:11

The band took a few weeks off to relax before commencing the songwriting sessions for the upcoming album. This time around, our comanager Bud Prager really got involved and wanted to take the songwriting to the next level of mainstream. This appealed to all of our egos, but I could see the rub inside Dave.

At his core, Dave is anything but mainstream in the traditional sense, and any success we ever had was mostly because of our genre and our fans—not because of some mastermind from the outside, which Bud was becoming. We were being prodded by Bud to take Megadeth in a musical direction that haunted the band and its fans for the next decade. As metal music was being reinvented via the nu-metal movement of the late 1990s, we were writing in a more melodic vein,

ultimately moving in the opposite direction. As our subsequent manager Larry Mazer later told us, we zigged when the rest of the world
zagged. Touché!

Relations soon became strained within the band and management. We were trying to hit a target toward which management
aimed us, but which we couldn't even see. One day Julie and I invited
Bud to our house so we could talk about money, songwriting, and
other basic tenets of Megadeth as it now existed. He and I sat on the
couch in our living room and he basically said to me, "Be happy
you're even here." He went on to explain that Dave was like Bruce
Springsteen, and that the rest of us should stop trying to write songs
and be happy that we had the talent of Dave in the band, as he was
our meal ticket.

My heart sank. Were these the discussions he was having with
Dave? Was this the banter of the band room when I wasn't there? What
was hilarious was that Bud obviously regarded what he was saying as a
pep talk. He later told me that if the album was a success, Dave would
be considered a genius, but if it flopped then he, Bud, would be considered the bad guy. When the album, *Risk*, flopped, I made him eat his
own words, although all these years later, I bear Bud—who passed
away in 2008—no ill will.

The lesson I learned here was that it was a professional move,
rather than one to take personally. However, business can be personal,
especially in the creative realm of a band—and even more so when the
band members are required to live together on the road. After discussions like the one I'd had with Bud, with someone who isn't even on
the road with you, nothing is easy.

We headed to Nashville once more to begin the recording of *Risk*,
again with Dann Huff at the helm, but on our arrival we realized that
the songs were incomplete. As a result, we spent a lot of time writing
songs in the studio, paying extremely high daily rates. I had to learn
new songs and new parts and basically write my lines on the spot,
which was not a method I was used to at all. Even the bass guitar tones

were mostly Fenderesque, with a much more organic and less metal sound.

Personally, I was just looking forward to playing my bass parts and simply getting out of there, given the stress we were dealing with. At the end of the day, it was a record that by and large was not even our idea. It was hands down the most uncomfortable session of my entire career.

It didn't help that since *Cryptic Writings*, Dann had produced several chart-topping records with country superstars Keith Urban and Faith Hill. He mentioned to me that *Risk* would be the last rock record he could afford to make. In his mind, he could churn out a country record in four to six weeks, which would sell millions, as opposed to taking five months to make a rock record, in a genre where sales were declining. *Risk* was the last album we did with Dann.

What scared me most was that I saw a repeating pattern over our career of one album, such as our debut record, followed by a more successful follow-up. Then the next album would be less successful, and the next one after that would turn the tide again. I had seen this happen over and over again. If the pattern held, *Risk* would be a stiff, not a success.

I thought *Risk* was a good album, but I also thought that it shouldn't have had Megadeth's name on it. People had a certain expectation about what Megadeth was supposed to sound like, and this certainly wasn't it. The album completely failed to live up to the brand. Of course, it was a strange time for all the main thrash metal bands. Metallica had taken a lot of heat for cutting their hair and altering their music, and we were heading the same way.

My own image changed, I'll admit. I remember shooting a video in 1997 for the song "Trust" from the previous album, *Cryptic Writings*, while wearing a pair of $4,000 leather trousers, and feeling a little at odds with myself. Roman had just been born and I didn't want him to think that I was just some old curmudgeonly biker guy. I felt as if I should suit up like a real dad, so one day I just shaved my hair off. It looked like crap anyway, now that we were living out in Arizona. Somehow the dry heat and water was making my hair look a mess, not full, as it had been in California. In a way, cutting my hair in 1997 was the breath of fresh air that enabled me to re-create and start over—not an easy task in the public spotlight, and even less so in the face of criticism from fans.

We headed out on the road, but venues were smaller. We mostly played theaters and a few grimy clubs. A regime change had occurred at Capitol Records since the success of *Cryptic Writings*, and with the less-than-favorable sales out of the gate for *Risk*, more stress mounted between us and the label. I remember they came to our House of Blues show in Los Angeles and gave us a plaque to celebrate 500,000 copies sold around the world. We used to sell that many in the U.S. alone, and usually within the first month.

Times were changing, and financial stress was looming. We owed Capitol one more album, however, so I tried to do my usual diplomatic thing of keeping everyone's hopes high. I pointed out that at least we still had a major-label deal, at a time when traditional thrash metal was in the toilet—and many bands of our genre were scrambling just to survive.

A jam backstage with Megadeth's webmaster set us all thinking a little about the direction we were going in.

Dave McRobb (Megadeth.com webmaster): I remember jamming with the guys in November 1999. I knew them already because I was a moderator on the Megadeth online forum, and I'd won a contest through the website to play with them backstage in Quebec City [Canada], where they were playing a show. I was playing guitar and we jammed some songs from *Rust in Peace.* One of them was "Lucretia," which they probably hadn't played since the album came out. Ellefson was sitting beside me on the couch, and the two of us had a lot of fun trying to remember how the song went. I remember Marty sitting across from me and ripping into the solo. It was really cool for me to get to do that, as a fan. After that I got more involved with the band's website, and I ultimately became the webmaster in 2003.

Tensions within the band finally reached the boiling point following a long and heated discussion on the tour bus after a show in Philadelphia. As we headed down to Myrtle Beach, North Carolina, Dave was emphatic that we take our musical direction back to thrash metal. To his credit, he didn't want to pretend to be a pop band any longer. I'll never forget what was said next: I was sitting on the couch in the right front lounge and Marty was by the refrigerator, when he flatly stated, "If that's the direction we're going in, then I'm out," and went to bed. The silence was deafening.

I wasn't sure that I wanted to go back to old-school thrash metal at that point either. I didn't know what I wanted. On one level I felt as if we should evolve, that as humans we should grow in new directions. I liked playing the slower songs in big halls to huge audiences. But those days were at an end and a change was needed. That was clear to all of us.

The next day Dave called me in my hotel room to inform me Marty had quit Megadeth. We were both stunned. What was happening to our band?

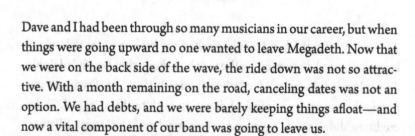

Marty Friedman (former Megadeth guitarist): Ellefson understood my reasons for leaving Megadeth. I didn't sense any hard feelings from him, then or later. It was really cool of him to look past the fact that I left Megadeth at a bad time.

Dave and I had been through so many musicians in our career, but when things were going upward no one wanted to leave Megadeth. Now that we were on the back side of the wave, the ride down was not so attractive. With a month remaining on the road, canceling dates was not an option. We had debts, and we were barely keeping things afloat—and now a vital component of our band was going to leave us.

We knew that the fans' reaction wasn't going to be good. As good as Jimmy DeGrasso was, many Megadeth fans already missed the *Rust in Peace* lineup, which had featured Nick Menza. Without Marty, the fallout would be even worse. The team was disintegrating, but we had no choice except to soldier on. Jimmy was the consummate professional, and failure was not an option in his book either. He quickly recommended Al Pitrelli as an immediate substitute for Marty so that we could carry on with the live dates.

At the same time, we were engaging in our first real corporate sponsorship with stereo equipment manufacturer JVC. Who knew what they would do if they saw the chink in our armor caused by Marty leaving? Our first real test was a JVC corporate acoustic show in Las Vegas in early 2000. We flew Al out to watch us play, and he came to my hotel room after the show so that we could sit down and start the process of learning the eighteen-song live set. As good as Al was, he was a long way from being able to pull off Marty's guitar parts on such short notice, let alone produce true thrash metal playing. He was a rock 'n' roll gunslinger, not a dyed-in-the-wool metal guy.

Fortunately, Marty agreed to stay on board for a couple more weeks, working with Al each day on the bus to help break him in. I also sat down with Al and worked through the arrangements, as I had always done with new members. Never before had Al been in a band that understood the essential role of picking-hand palm muting in thrash metal. But Al is a fantastic musician, and he really stepped up under the pressure.

In fact, Al's debut with Megadeth came sooner than he expected. Marty, who had been flying to all the shows separately from the rest of the band now, suffered what appeared to be an anxiety attack at one point, demanding that we get another guitarist in immediately. Al was almost ready, but not quite. Marty was supposed to play his final show with us on January 16, 2000, at the Commodore Ballroom in Vancouver, but as the clock drew closer to showtime, there was no sign of Marty. Half an hour before we were supposed to go on, Dave looked at Al and told him to lace up his boots and get ready to hit the stage.

The show went off well—the band sounded heavier than it had in years. This final transition of both Marty and Nick out of the group needed to happen, in retrospect. Al and Jimmy had a much more behind-the-beat style of playing, which anchored the band more than it had ever been before. As a bassist, I loved it. We were developing a new sound. It was invigorating, and once more, we were back to me and Dave plus two new guys.

We continued to tour through 2000, playing dates with Mötley Crüe and Anthrax for the Maximum Rock tour of North America. It was an odd mix, and as if the poor reception of *Risk* hadn't been enough, now we were really out on the edge with live fan reach. Although it was still better than the ill-fated Aerosmith tour of 1993, the Mötley tour was greeted with poor ticket sales. Tommy Lee was not in the band at the time, and the situation was disjointed on their side as well.

A stroke of good fortune lay ahead, however. Our manager Mike Renault had been shopping for a new record deal for the band and brought in an amazing offer from Sanctuary Records, a part of the Iron Maiden and Rod Smallwood camp. Sanctuary was mostly an indie conglomerate, and we knew we probably weren't going to sell anywhere close to the numbers we would need to recoup the advance in the deal. However, the deal was rich and it was certainly a draw for us.

To Dave's credit, as much as we've both experienced the "feast or famine" side of the music business, he's never considered the money first in any decisions he's made for the band. In fact, he has always made the music and the execution of the band our top priorities, which in turn has helped keep the money flowing. I'm not as good with that, so it is a lesson I've tried to learn from him: do what you love and the money will follow. *Risk* may have been a lesson to all of us that when you put the attraction of success before the actual success comes, you have placed the cart before the horse.

We were now seriously disheartened with Bud Prager. It was sad, because our point man Mike Renault was a hard worker, and he had resolved some of the precarious financial debt and upside-down business management that had been a part of the Youthanasia tour cycle. Our tour manager Steve Wood had previously worked with ace rock manager Larry Mazer, based in the Cherry Hill area of New Jersey, just outside Philadelphia. I knew of Larry's track record with breaking Cinderella in the 1980s, as well as his work with KISS and Pat Benatar.

Steve had Larry come to a show on the Mötley Crüe tour in Camden, New Jersey, where he gave us his full pitch about why he should be our new manager. His "Go team, go!" approach fell on eager ears and within a few weeks we had fired Bud and Mike and hired Larry. I liked Mike and hated to see him go. Bud was a different story, not because I disliked him as a man, but rather because he pulled the divide-and-conquer routine on the band during *Risk*.

Larry put the Sanctuary deal in place for us, and after the Mötley Crüe tour we went back to Dave's studio, where we had written *Risk*, and started to carve out the songs for what would become our next album, *The World Needs a Hero*. This was a title based on a conversation our Japanese promoter Mr. Udo had had with us over dinner one night, at the end of the Cryptic Writings tour in late 1998. Dave liked the idea, and it became a reality.

We found a good engineer in Bill Kennedy, who had coincidentally just worked with Mötley Crüe. Bill didn't have much creative input into the music, though, as this was Dave's time to try and turn Megadeth back into the thrash metal icon it deserved to be. However, it was like turning a giant ocean liner on the open seas—one spin of the wheel takes a long time to make any difference. So it was with *The World Needs a Hero*, which only made a minor dent in our major issues.

I thought the album was okay, and a lot better than *Risk*. It was the first step away from the direction in which Megadeth had been going, but we hadn't focused entirely on writing thrash metal songs. We were writing choruses, as we had been for most of the previous ten years, and it's hard to switch back to writing riffs from that approach.

The album was released by Sanctuary, even though it was technically our final album for Capitol. VH1 filmed a *Behind the Music* special about Megadeth, where we all talked about sobriety and how great things were going for us. I think Dave especially liked that he was able to talk about his Metallica years, and James Hetfield and Lars Ulrich even agreed to be interviewed in the episode. It was my job, as the diplomat, to reach out to the former members to participate. After much coaxing on my part, Jeff Young and Chris Poland agreed to take part, too. I was happy for them as the program gave them some public visibility and a platform to talk about their experiences in the band.

We set up *The World Needs a Hero* with a three-week acoustic tour across the U.S. where we would do local radio during the day and perform in a 500- to 1,000-seat theater that evening. This was a great way to play an intimate show for our fans while at the same time schmoozing the radio folks for Sanctuary—all part of a game that we were well-versed in playing by this point.

We toured the festivals in Europe that summer, then played Japan and Korea, before moving down the Pacific Rim to Indonesia, Australia, and New Zealand. We then agreed to a 1,000-capacity club tour in the fall as a way to set our guarantees of money. This also meant that we didn't have to spend so much on a costly production to keep the machine on the road.

We had a day off on September 10, 2001, and I went to the local cinema to chill out. I watched the movies *American Pie* and *Rock Star* and went back to the hotel to get some sleep. The next morning, before 6 A.M., Dave called and woke me up to tell me that a plane had crashed into the World Trade Center towers in New York City. Thirty minutes later the second plane hit the towers and it felt as if we were in a world war.

Our show in Seattle was canceled that night, but we made our way across the border into Vancouver, Canada, for the show next day. It was freaky to leave your own country when all the planes were grounded, without much knowledge of what had just happened, but as they say in this business, the show must go on.

We played our final shows of the World Needs a Hero tour in Tucson and Phoenix on November 16 and 17. Those shows became the *Rude Awakening* live DVD and double CD set. While the shows looked and sounded good, I was thoroughly baked from it all. I was extremely ill with chronic asthma and bronchitis for most of 2001, from the pressures of band-member and management changes.

These past few years were really starting to take a toll, and I was seriously pondering what life outside the band might look like for me. Add to that, the mood in the U.S. had been dark since the 9/11 attacks. This forced us to make Arizona our final shows on the tour, rather than the originally intended Buenos Aires for the grand finale.

In my mind, things had become a mess. Al had pulled me aside two weeks prior in Denver to tell me he was quitting the band and going back to Trans-Siberian Orchestra, his previous home before he joined Megadeth. He actually offered me an audition to play on the upcoming TSO tour that year, but I was fried from all the touring and declined. It would have been fun, because musically Al and I were a good match. Had I known what was to follow, I would have taken him up on his offer. Sometimes taking a leap of faith is the best course of action, a lesson with which I'd soon become acquainted.

I was sitting in church one day, pondering how I had been told in rehab that everything would have to change in order for my development as a sober person to take place. It occurred to me that everything had in fact changed in my life, with the exception of one thing: Megadeth. The end was coming, though, and sooner than I had expected. After filming those last two shows for *Rude Awakening*, Dave injured his arm and informed us that he was officially quitting Megadeth. This was February 4, 2002.

After receiving that phone call I went out to the backyard of my home in Scottsdale. My first thought was "Now what am I supposed to do with my life?" followed by a huge sigh of relief that it was over. Julie and I were looking for a bigger house at the time, somewhere that would be more suited to our growing family and my home studio and office needs. The timing couldn't have been worse. I had thought that the Sanctuary deal would have secured a nice retirement for us. Julie and I even discussed moving to New Jersey, to be close to her parents, but Dave asked me not to do that in case he needed my help. But it was not to be.

I was devastated. At the same time, I was relieved to not have to be around the drama of a rock band anymore. I was tired of living under the pretense that I had to be in a touring rock band while facing the realities of being a father in a loving family, who really needed my time at home. It was time for me to grow up once and for all. Within minutes the strangest thing happened: the chronic asthma from which I had suffered the year before suddenly disappeared. It was as if the weight of the world was finally off my chest. Dave had done for me what I couldn't do for myself, which is quit.

Dave told me that he wanted to assign the catalog to me, so we met in a Starbucks by my house in Scottsdale. He had a stack of paperwork with him detailing the catalog from Capitol Records, which he wanted me to remaster and reissue. My heart wasn't in it, though. I knew that if Megadeth no longer worked, I wouldn't have an income to sustain my family. I had to move on to new endeavors as the breadwinner of my home. I was very freaked out and still in a state of shock, and I now knew what Marty felt like when he was done. I told Dave, "Thank you for giving me the opportunity to live out my dream," meaning, "Thank you for our partnership over the years."

As the day went on, however, I became more and more angry with his decision to leave the group, and after seeing him at a meeting a few hours later I angrily told him, "If you're getting on with your life, then I'm getting on with mine." They were very harsh, tense words and I got in my car and drove off.

A THOUGHT

Change—The Ultimate Leap of Faith

While change can be liberating, it can also be scary. Ironically, my life in a rock 'n' roll band was nothing but constant change, and I experienced it together with my band of brothers. But when change comes upon you without asking for it, that is a whole other story. Especially when this first big change of my adult life made me question everything I had known from the previous eighteen years, as a member of a successful heavy metal band.

Fortunately, God seems to make a way when there seems to be no other way. Those were the moments when all I had to back me up was hope that it would somehow work out, and faith that it actually would. Seemingly, that was all that was required to start a new life.

CHAPTER ELEVEN

Transformed

> "If any of you has a dispute with another, do you dare to take it before the ungodly for judgment instead of before the Lord's people?"
>
> —1 Corinthians 6:1

As I look back on my life so far, it's pretty clear to me that when I unhooked myself from the train of consequences that was Megadeth, I embarked on a new journey that was sober, mature, responsible, stable, and, finally, adult.

The first thing I did was start looking for jobs. Fender had called me about a possible bass amp product manager job, which I wasn't really equipped for. Also they wanted me in the office full-time, with no time for any future tours. At this exact same time, Alice Cooper's camp called to ask if I wanted to play bass with them for an upcoming tour. As much as I appreciated Alice's offer, I also realized that I needed to be with my family during this season of my life, as I might very well wake up on a tour bus at the age of fifty, and have completely missed my kids growing up. I had to stay the course of being responsible for providing for my family, even if that meant sacrificing my dreams of music and rock stardom.

I then considered a career as a producer, but I didn't relish the idea of being stuck in a studio for the rest of my life. I did, however, produce three songs for the band Numm out of Minneapolis, which included a friend of mine, Dale Steele, in their lineup. Nothing happened with that band or the demos, though. I wasn't sure if I was cut out for a career flying around the country, producing unsigned bands. I also spoke to Monte Conner at Roadrunner Records, investigating an A&R role with them, and that didn't materialize either, but Roadrunner did ask me to go and do some writing with their band Dry Kill Logic. This was an eye-opening experience for me, musically and with the music business. By and large it helped me open up dialogues with current record companies, managers, agents, and publishers.

At this time there was a wave of modern heavy metal where all the bands tuned down, which was a different sound from that of traditional metal bands like Megadeth who tuned to the standard concert pitch of A440. It was funny writing with the Dry Kill Logic guys, who were all ten years younger than me, tuned down to A# and all these other whacked-out tunings. All of a sudden I realized that I was the old guy in the room. I got hip to the sound, though, because it was really a great thing to be exposed to.

All the old rules of thrash metal, which I'd lived with, had gone out the window, and it was so liberating. I started breaking out my old riff tapes of unused material from as far back as *Countdown to Extinction* and playing them in a new tuning, and they sounded completely fresh. I had a whole new palette of creativity on the same fingerboard that I'd been playing for twenty years. It was like learning to paint all over again.

But apart from those inspirations, I felt as if I had nothing going on career-wise with any real substance or momentum. I was really angry about it all and not a pleasant guy to be around during this time. I felt as if my whole rock star dream had been taken away from me. I know it sounds selfish, because to most, I had already achieved the dream. But I struggled with the reality that the decision to change my life had been made for me, rather than something that I had a hand in, and that bothered me. I knew that playing music professionally was still my calling, and I'd certainly laid the groundwork for a successful legacy. The trick was doing it while still being able to provide for my family. There were a lot of growing pains during this period and I just had to man up and deal with them.

My marriage was put under some strain, because there were now financial issues and because my whole identity was different. Previously, any time a kid in a heavy metal T-shirt came up to me in a grocery store and asked for an autograph, I'd go into rock star mode. Now I wasn't a star anymore, and had to work like everybody else. It was tough for my ego, I'll admit, although it was refreshing to drop all the celebrity airs and go back to being the salt-of-the-earth guy from the farm that I used to be. It was a great ideal, but sometimes a difficult reality.

Finally, after consulting with record labels on A&R jobs and producing, I considered another behind-the-scenes role in the industry, that of artist relations for a musical instrument manufacturer. I had dealt with many of the people in these positions for my own endorsements, so I felt that a role on the other side of the corporate desk might be a good fit for me.

I called a buddy who formerly worked for Ampeg, a brand I had previously used on the *Youthanasia* cycle. His name was Tony Moscal and he was now working with Peavey. Coincidentally, I was currently endorsed by Peavey for my bass amplification. Suddenly, I felt a surge of hope.

Tony made the referral for me, and Peavey's president, Mary Peavey, called me up and said they were very excited about the possibility of working with me, which put a spring in my step, because until that moment I'd really felt like a man without a country. I flew down to meet with Mary and Tony for my interview, which back then involved part of the trip flying on a small and turbulent turboprop plane to arrive at their headquarters in Meridian, Mississippi. Mind you, this was something of a change for a guy who had been accustomed to flying around the world in jumbo jets, either business or first class, for the past fifteen years.

I arrived at Peavey and the owner, Hartley Peavey, had his own aircraft hangar, which was impressive. I think they liked that they were hiring a guy who had been around the world and knew the industry. By the way, this was the first time I had ever prepared a résumé! I made a three- or four-page document with everything on it that I had ever done professionally, and apart from the creative side it struck me that pretty much everything I'd done as a rock star could be summed up as marketing, whether it was promoting the band through interviews, Internet promotions, and so on. I really had a knack for marketing, it seemed, although I'd always looked with disdain upon salesmen and these slimy corporate marketing guys who I'd see at trade shows and the like. My view of them was about to change.

My job with Peavey was to go out and prepare artists to endorse their products. It was basically a cell-phone-and-laptop job, which I did from my home in Arizona, but I took it as seriously as if I were actually there in the office. I'd wake up in the morning and check in with Peavey HQ, whatever the time was according to the one- or two-hour time difference, and get on with my daily tasks. It was an interesting job, because Peavey was an established brand and they wanted to build a much higher profile for their amplifiers and guitars in conjunction with artist endorsements.

I started reaching out to artists as clients and it was gratifying, because they all took my calls. I guess I'd never realized how popular and influential Megadeth was, or that I enjoyed so much respect from so many people, because I'd been in an internationally famous band for so long. It taught me that the only way to really lose is to give up. As long as you stay in the game, in any line of work, you can become well known for it and respected, too.

So here I was, doing a lot of cold calling to management companies, agents, and even record labels. Some of the first artists I brought on board were Paul Gray from Slipknot, Mike Kroeger from Nickelback, the keyboard player for Kid Rock, and a few other pretty big fish, all within the first few months.

Mike Kroeger (Nickelback): We were looking around for a new amp company, and my tech came in and said he had David Ellefson on the phone. I said "What? Why have you got the bass player from Megadeth on the phone?" and he said, "He works for Peavey now and wants to know if you'd like to try some of their gear." I said, "Yes. I'd love to try their stuff!" It turned out that Peavey's amps were awesome. I'd been in other situations with bass and amp manufacturers where their staff were overwhelmed and unable to do their job, because they had one guy doing the job of four or five people and they couldn't possibly do it all properly, but Ellefson made time for me and came out to the shows. He was a really great guy and always had a word of encouragement for us.

I didn't have a target to hit. Instead, I just went for it with all the gusto I had, eager to prove that I could do it, both to myself and to Peavey. I had a new role in life and I really liked it. I was now esteemed as the artist-relations manager for one of the largest musical manufacturers in the world, and I reported to Tony, who was a tremendous mentor to me throughout the process. I owe a lot to him, and to Peavey, for taking a chance on me. Tony had a famous artist-relations manager over at Ampeg, keyboardist Ken Hensley of Uriah Heep, so Tony was very hip to the dynamics of this "famous guy doing endorsements for a company" thing. He knew that a well-known musician like me from a credible band like Megadeth who was actually using the company's products professionally, in charge of talking to artists, could only be helpful for Peavey. It worked out very well. It was definitely a successful method of doing business.

Once the Peavey gig was locked in, Julie and I once again considered moving to New Jersey, but ultimately we decided that we wanted Roman and Athena to stay at their Christian school in Arizona. It was the right decision, because my whole life had recently been turned completely upside down and we wanted to buffer them from the impact of that change. It was beautiful to work at home doing the artist-relations job. I could stay plugged into my local recovery community and keep the kids in their school. It was a great job and, to me, a gift from God.

I had to make this work. My annual income had dropped to around a quarter of what it had been in Megadeth, which as anyone who supports a family will know is a serious blow. I had some investments and savings, but I wasn't financially secure by any means.

I was basically a guy who had lost a really good, high-paying corporate job. That's how I looked at it, because Megadeth was a corporate rock band by that point. The Sanctuary deal was supposed to have kept us all going through 2002, but of course that money didn't exist as long as the group was disbanded. At the same time, there was no threat to my sobriety. I wasn't about to fall off the wagon and undo all the work I'd done because my band didn't exist anymore. It turns out that the years of daily discipline had cemented a foundation for me.

Let me say this. It's almost as if I'd been given the grace of all those years clean to prepare me for these changes. I knew in my gut that God hadn't given me the twelve years of sobriety that I had amassed at the time just to yank the rug out from under me. This phase was just the beginning of a new and exciting chapter, and I had faith that the good Lord would provide. Besides, everything in this world will eventually leave you. You'll either let go of it or it will be taken from you, but sooner or later everything will be removed.

You come into this world alone, and you go out of it alone, and the journey of your life is really about your relationship with your Creator, and how you can fit into the scheme of life as He would have it be. God was doing for me what I couldn't do for myself—He was guiding me onto new pathways of life, toward experiences that would shape me into a better person and bring me closer to Him, too.

To me, the book in your hands is about transformations, both good and bad, but there are no mistakes in God's world. After Megadeth was swept away and I felt like a man with no country, ultimately these became the best things that ever happened to me. Eventually, I found a real peace and my creativity was invigorated.

I look back on this time as some of the happiest years of my life, but the initial stages were tough. I went through a long period of grief, of emptiness and anger. Unfortunately, I took a lot of that anger out on my wife, not because she deserved it but because she happened to be the closest person around at the time. Luckily, she remained a calm voice of reason. I'd been sober a long time, and I kept the faith that it would work out if I rolled up my sleeves, got to work, and really put my faith in God to carry me through.

It did work out, of course. I was really getting on with my life now. I had to suit up and show up every day, and what I found was that I was resourceful enough as a person to do that. Unlike with Megadeth, where the money was good but the demands were often small in that all they required of me was a couple of hours a day, now my day was completely different. It was invigorating. My mind was fired up, and I was creatively charged. I began to realize that I was going to be okay.

Despite the reduced income, all my bills were paid and my family's needs were seen to. As a bonus, after a year or so the Megadeth catalog recouped its advances and royalty checks started showing up.

Did I miss being the center of attention onstage? Sure, at the beginning. But I knew from my recovery work that the greatest rewards in life come from serving, not from being served. That's what we do in recovery: we prepare a place for fellowship, especially for those in need. Best I can tell, those of us that have the most successful lives do not base them on the size of our tax returns or how many cars we have in the garage. Instead, our lives are built on inner peace, which results from honest self-appraisal, housecleaning of old ways, and continued service to others. I was okay with putting "David Ellefson from Megadeth" to one side and introducing myself on the phone as "David Ellefson from Peavey." I was playing on a big field now called corporate America, and it suited my personality perfectly.

Of course, there were some interesting contrasts, one of which came when I rolled into the NAMM show of 2003. NAMM sponsors a huge trade conference held in Anaheim, California, every January to showcase new innovations in guitars, basses, keyboards, drums, amps, and other technologies.

The NAMM shows are executed on an extremely large scale, second only in size to the Musikmesse in Frankfurt, Germany. NAMM is always full of rock and metal fans, and they were constantly coming up to me asking when Megadeth was going to re-form, and how Dave's arm was. I couldn't really answer these questions in the way they wanted, of course. My job was to keep my head down, learn how NAMM operated from the inside, and work hard for Peavey. But they kept coming at me, because I was completely exposed to the general public in the Peavey trade show booth. At the end of the show we had to take the gear apart and put it all on pallets to be taken back to Mississippi. It was quite a workload, seeing as I hadn't set up or torn down gear in maybe fifteen years! I'd had roadies and stagehands to handle those duties for most of my career.

But I didn't resent my change of status. I was in my late thirties at this point, married with two children, sober for thirteen years, and there was a wisdom in me to know that the rock star life was the dream of a teenager. The product you're selling is mostly a fantasy. It's not really a song or a T-shirt; it's "Don't you wish you could be like me?" That's an immature product from the viewpoint of someone who is heading toward forty.

My Peavey gig was a reprieve from rock 'n' roll. It was a spiritual steroid, if you will, and it enabled me to recalibrate and take stock of my life. It also enabled me to be an example to my children. As a parent, I realized that the impact I made on my children would be more important than the satisfaction I got from rock 'n' roll.

That NAMM show was crucial, because it showed me that I could survive it. Every subsequent NAMM show was the same. I was there to work for Peavey. At the same time, Megadeth's work was becoming more revered. Our early albums were now being looked upon as iconic. I also started to design some amps and basses for Peavey, one of which was a signature-series bass called the Zodiac series. I became more confident in my dual role as a rock star and employee. Some companies might not have welcomed that, but Peavey did.

At that time, Dave Small, a drummer friend from Phoenix, told me that he had been playing with a local guitarist I knew named Steve Conley. I had produced some demos for a band Steve was in called Lifted, which I really liked, so I went over to his house with my bass and played on a track for him. He was initially going to use that track as an audition for a position in the band Halford, fronted by Judas Priest's lead singer.

The vibe with Steve and Dave was fun, so I went back a couple of weeks later and started playing with them again. That was the day that a new band, F5, was born. Two or three song ideas came immediately. We came up with the band name when Small was watching the movie *Twister*. F5 was the name of the huge tornados, "the fingers of God," as they are known. We had such an explosive, creative vibe, even though I had said that I would never put another band together again.

I knew how much hard work it would be to put a band together, and I knew exactly what issues would follow, but I still enjoyed performing. The Good Lord intended me to have a guitar or a bass in my hand, and I loved playing with F5. It was really the first time that I felt validated for my musical ideas, too.

I was on a new path in my life and now a new band was starting to form around me. It was a true labor of love—we rehearsed two or three times a week and it was very exciting. The guys were all younger than me, with a more modern ear. They tuned their guitars down, like the guitarists in Dry Kill Logic had, and, as before, when I suggested ideas that I'd come up with in the '90s, they sounded totally modern.

The only obstacle I recall came when our first show was booked. It was all ready to go, but I put the brakes on it, suddenly realizing that it was the first show I'd played post-Megadeth. The reality hit me. If I was going to take it to the stage, I wanted it to be great. This slowed F5's trajectory at first. It probably would have been good for us to go out and play a few club shows rather than me trying to launch it as this big project. Despite this, F5 had an album's worth of songs and JVC in Japan offered us a recording deal.

I also began to work with Billy Smiley, the guitar player and songwriter of a big Christian group called Whiteheart. I had met him in Nashville on the last day of my bass overdubs on the *Risk* album. He was moving to Scottsdale at the time. I connected with him three years later and we became friends. He came to my house the day after Megadeth ended, and told me to get back up on the horse and ride, and to start writing new songs. It was fantastic that he did that. We recorded an album together under the name Symphony in Red, which rearranged hymns for rock bands, similar to what Trans-Siberian Orchestra does with Christmas songs. I played with Billy for the next few years, doing sessions on and off, mostly in Nashville. One of them was an album by famed Christian artist Scott Wesley Brown, called *The Old Made New*, which is still one of my favorites of the albums I've played on because of the lyrical content. I put it on when I'm driving in my car and it just feels good, a very inspirational record.

As F5 began in early 2003, my name was suggested to Soulfly as a possible bass player. I went down to see them at the Marquee Theatre in Tempe, and they were really good. Primer 55 guitarist Bobby Burns was playing bass and the guitarist Marc Rizzo was amazing. I spoke to their manager, Gloria Cavalera, and told her that I'd be happy to record and tour with them if they ever needed me, and so she decided that Bobby and I would both play on the next album, *Prophecy*. It was a very fun session, and very creative.

Soulfly's singer, Max Cavalera, was a great guy to play with. The album was just about the most relaxed metal session I've ever been a part of. Max didn't dictate the bass parts to me: he had hired me to do what I did, and so he let me have complete free rein for everything. I had total liberty with the bass parts and I was very creative with them, which was very different from Megadeth, where many times bass parts were written for me as part of the overall composition or production. It was two completely different schools of thought.

Max Cavalera (Soulfly): David is a great guy, and he kicked butt on the songs he did. We did the "Prophecy" video with him, and we played a couple of weeks' worth of shows together. The crowd really liked him, and for a little while there was a kind of supergroup feel. He is such a great bass player. I really enjoyed playing with him. You can tell when you're playing with a professional, and he was always a pro—a real musician.

It wasn't the right time to join Soulfly full-time, although I did enjoy my experience with them. I was still fairly new in my Peavey position, and that was a steady job I could do at home. If I'd gone out on tour with Soulfly for long periods, I doubt I would have been able to keep it. The Peavey gig provided security and stability for my family, and it also allowed me to work with F5. As long as I could get my job done I could tour, although I never wanted to be away for more than a couple of weeks, for ethical reasons. I wanted to be home and be a good example for my kids. I was able to attend my kids' sporting events at school and so on—which wouldn't have been possible had I still been a member of a full-time touring band.

I did play two weeks of shows with Soulfly, though. Bobby Burns had suffered a minor stroke and Gloria called me and said, "Can you be in San Diego on Monday?" She had Dan Lilker come in to fill in after me. Soulfly with me in it sounded great. It was really heavy, and there was a great musical kinship and camaraderie among us. We played really well together. I'd experimented with lower tunings in F5, so I was accustomed to that approach in Soulfly. In fact, most of the things I did away from Megadeth were in unusual tunings.

I was recording the *Prophecy* album with Soulfly when all of a sudden Dave called me and said, "Hey, I'm ready to play again." It wasn't the first time we'd spoken since the split: we'd had a couple of conversations, but they were not friendly, because when I declined Dave's offer to manage the Megadeth catalog, it meant that Dave had to handle all the collateral damage himself. However, I was genuinely thrilled to hear from him.

I met him in Starbucks again, on Ninety-Second Street and Shea, by our homes in Scottsdale, where we had had many Megadeth meetings. He called me two days later and said that Sanctuary were interested in resuming their deal with us, and I assumed that we would simply pick up business again right where we had left off. However, the terms were that this time everything would be completely rearranged, with my participation and reward only a fraction of what it had previously been. As Dave has stated, it was initially hoped that the project would be his solo record, not a band album. It was almost as if I was being offered the position back in the band as a legal obligation.

I declined the offer and a short while later I decided to launch a lawsuit. The suit was specifically designed to drive both parties back to the negotiating table. It was simply a matter of a member leaving the band, rather than any kind of corporate meltdown. It was mishandled, however, and in many ways not something I really wanted to do, even though there I was, smack-dab in the middle of the whole thing.

What I learned from it was that you can win a battle and ultimately lose the war. It strained the relationship between Dave and me, and it divided the fans, because that's what happens when you go through a nasty breakup like that. I didn't sleep for nine months while it was going on, because taking this kind of aggressive legal action is not in my nature.

If I had to do it all over again, I would never have filed the suit. I would simply have driven over to Dave's house, discussed it with him, agreed to the deal, and then simply had the attorneys handle the legalese. But I had to go through this as a learning process, and the terms to which we ultimately agreed were better, if not hugely so, than the original terms I'd been offered.

Time does heal wounds, for sure, and after a little while you gain some perspective and you realize that you should be thankful for a lot of things. I learned to follow my instincts, and when my instincts said no to the lawsuit, I should have listened. I had a record deal with F5 and my life starting to blossom in a whole new direction. I was building self-confidence. I'd moved away from Megadeth being my only identity and I could stand up for myself. That in itself was a good thing.

As soon as the lawsuit was settled, I enrolled in college for a two-year course to finish my bachelor's degree in business. I continued to work for Peavey, certain that my life with Megadeth was over.

A THOUGHT

Politics Leads to Religion

Most of us have a political stance on any given subject. It's our God-given right as humans to have opinions. I generally consider myself to be a liberal-minded person with a "live and let live" mind-set, which has developed from traveling the world all these years. When you see people from other cultures with beliefs different from yours, it reminds you that there may be more than one way to do things in this world. In short, keeping an open mind has helped me to be tolerant of other people and their lives.

While I've never taken my political beliefs into the public arena, one of my primary motivations for reading the Bible as an adult was perpetuated because I continually saw a "moral majority" conveniently aligning themselves with political parties of the same belief, somehow insinuating that if you belonged to a certain political party you needed to be Christian, and vice versa. Well, I'm not cut from that cloth, so I had to get some answers.

I set out to do some discovery of my own, and that was really my initial motivation to read the Bible, to gain my own understanding of what was in it and to see if there were real political overtones in it or not. Ironically, much of what I discovered in the New Testament about Jesus is that he spent vast amounts of his ministry trying to liberate the people of his day from the restricted and legalistic views of the time. Too much law and not enough grace. I was actually relieved to learn this, because it answered my basic question about religion, politics, and Christianity. The bottom line is, I had to read the Bible to understand it. Rather than judge it for what I *thought* it said, I finally read it to know what it really *did* say.

With that understanding, I try my best to leave both politics and religion out of my public life, because as soon as you align with one side, you instantly alienate yourself from the other.

CHAPTER TWELVE

The Age of Reinvention

"Life is a lot like jazz—it's best when you improvise."
—George Gershwin

After F5 formed in 2003, I got a call from Don Salter, who owns the Saltmine Studios in the Phoenix area. He gave up the lifestyle of a commercial real estate mogul to go and live the dream of being in the music business. He did well enough in real estate to open his own studio. Don wanted me to transition into producing, because touring with a band is a young man's game. He told me that he knew a guitarist named Yan Leviathan, who had a band called Avian, and that he wanted me to come down and produce it. I went for it.

At Don's studio I produced Yan's record and played bass on it, thinking that maybe another swing at producing for hire might not be a bad thing. Getting paid to do something is very different from everyone expecting you to work for them on a spec deal, in the hopes that one day the money will come in from a record deal. I had been doing that my whole life with rock bands, and I wasn't going to start all over as a producer, especially this late in the game. This opportunity was different, because Yan had the concept and funds for the album, to be named *From the Depths of Time*. I brought F5's then-drummer Dave Small in to play on it. This taught me the value of having a deep reserve of resources in the music business.

In the business of entertainment, the depth of your phone book often determines your success, and all those years of being the diplomat was now paying off. As it turns out, I was a pretty resourceful person in my eight years away from Megadeth. I had a lot of contacts, but they meant nothing unless I was actually going to utilize them. There's a lot to be said for that, and there's a lesson there for everyone. Getting out of our comfort zones is a requirement if things are going to be different moving forward. Do the same thing, get the same thing; do something different, get something different.

Producing was not the right career choice for me at the time, though. After some time locked in the studio, I tend to get cabin fever and go stir crazy. I don't like sitting in a dark room all day when the sun is out: I'd rather be out among the living.

God bless Don Salter for getting me those producing jobs, but ultimately I didn't want to be the guy producing—I wanted to be the guy playing. Some people, like Ross Robinson and James Murphy, successfully went from being musicians to producers, but that was not for me.

After a while I came up with a baseline for considering offers of musicians or bands to work with. It was that, in order to say yes, I had to like the people, and I had to like the music. I didn't want to be in a situation where I didn't like one, the other, or both.

One of the big lessons I learned about networking is that it's nice to reach out to people when the chips are down, which I did with guys like Billy Smiley, who were very quick to reciprocate with all of their resources. However, the other part of it is that you can create really beneficial partnerships with people. That really became my modus operandi in 2002, and it remains that way to this day.

Now, let's talk about adult education. I had dipped my toe in the waters of academia with the University of Phoenix's online degree program back in 1998 while on the Cryptic Writings tour. I had never done any college courses whatsoever, and with the recent developments in online education I felt that it was something that I could at least try out while on tour.

My first go at it was during a tour of Japan in 1998. I took my laptop and printer with me and did my homework in my downtime away from the stage. These were the days before e-mail was used by the general population, so I would print out my homework in my hotel room and go down to the hotel reception to fax it to my professor back in the U.S. I really enjoyed it, and it piqued my interest in world history and business. I spent so much of my life flying around the globe making great money and living the life of a successful rock star and business owner, but without having the academic fundamentals under my belt. These initial courses built some of that self-esteem for me. However, due to excessive travel and family duties, I decided to put the endeavor on hold after two courses and suspended my studies.

Then, in 2005, I enrolled in an online bachelor's degree program in business administration and marketing through American InterContinental University (AIU) in Illinois, a course that was moderately intense because it was designed to be completed in two years. With legal matters behind me, and my head clear, I felt that this was the best time to step up and finally get that degree completed once and for all. Plus, from working with Peavey, I realized that most people in the corporate workforce hold some sort of college degree, which allows them to move up in the ranks.

I realized how lucky I was to have landed a job at a corporation like Peavey without a formal degree. I also knew that I would need a degree to continue earning the respect of other successful people in the corporate world. This qualification would put me on a level playing field with them and help ensure my employability moving forward. Playing in a rock band didn't require a degree, but life outside a band probably would.

More musical projects continued to occupy my time outside my Peavey gig. A call came to me from Jon Dette, who had played drums with Slayer in the mid-1990s. He knew a guitar player named Peter Scheithauer, whose real name was actually Pierre Mougenot, and they were forming a band called Killing Machine. I'd never heard of the band, but they were working on some music Jon told me was really good. James Rivera of Helstar was the singer.

I liked the music and told them to count me in, but first they wanted to launch another band called Temple of Brutality, with a singer named Todd Barnes. I recorded an album with them in about a week, and man, I had fun with them. The music had a kind of thrash metal groove and it was a great experience. It was like the old days of thrash metal up in Berkeley and San Francisco, real fun and rowdy music. I called my friends at Jägermeister and they gave us a slot on the Arch Enemy/Chimaira tour that year. The band bought a motor home so we could go out and do the dates. I really felt like my life was in danger sometimes because the lifestyle hadn't changed. It was like the Killing Is My Business . . . tour: everyone was partying, except me.

I don't care if people party, of course, as long as it doesn't screw up the productivity. The problem was really that I was in my forties and a seasoned musician, as opposed to a young guy who would be happy to tour at a basic level. I enjoyed the creativity, and the experience confirmed what I already knew, which was that being in Megadeth had been a very special experience indeed.

Killing Machine came right after Temple of Brutality, and I called Jimmy DeGrasso in to play drums, because I loved playing with Jimmy any time I could. We cut the tracks for the album *Metalmorphosis* in Los Angeles. It was a fun project to do. For me it was about the camaraderie as well as making a really cool power metal record. Juan Garcia from Abattoir and Agent Steel was in there, too, as were James, Jimmy,

Peter, and I. It was a great chance to get a band of friends together, and this really contributed to my development as a person, because I became a kind of leader from behind.

I wasn't the guy up front like the singer, or even the songwriter, but I put things together and rallied people, plus I had a big hand in putting the album together. I was becoming a guy who would help projects develop from behind the scenes, a role that suited me.

Just before Christmas 2005 Dave called me up and we met for dinner in Phoenix. We'd seen each other once before, right in the middle of our lawsuit, but not since then. I took the opportunity to apologize to him for taking the legal route. I told him that I'd been reading the Bible and that 1 Corinthians 6 talks about not bringing lawsuit against your fellow Christian believers, and that, rather than wage that kind of war in the courts of law, it is better to suffer your losses and move on. It was good. We talked and he sent me a text on the way home offering forgiveness.

A week later he phoned again and asked if I wanted to do some touch-ups on the bass parts for a live recording he was mixing, presumably on Megadeth's *That One Night: Live in Buenos Aires* DVD. I was on my way down to Nashville to play with Billy Smiley anyway, and I was also doing a lot of work for Peavey down there. I had opened up their Nashville artist-relations office, so this period was very productive for me on many fronts.

I was excited about working with Dave again, but I suffered a serious attack of bronchitis and asthma shortly afterward, which I still experienced from time to time. I had to go to the hospital because I couldn't breathe, and the doctor gave me some numbing medication, after making me sign a waiver in case I fell back into drug use. I couldn't do the Megadeth session after all. Thankfully, this wasn't the last time that opportunity came around.

About this time I got involved in another interesting gig, with Montrose. Jimmy DeGrasso and I played with them in 2006 and 2007. Ricky Phillips, formerly of the Babys, had been playing bass with Montrose, but he got the call to go and join Styx, and Montrose's subsequent bassist was going off to play full-time with Pat Benatar, so they didn't have a bass player. They had one headlining show and two gigs coming up with Def Leppard; one down in Jacksonville, Florida, and another out in Alabama. So Jimmy said, "You should do it," and I said, "Okay, I'm in."

I talked to Ronnie Montrose and he wanted to know if I could groove, despite being a heavy metal guy. I said, "Don't worry, I can groove. I know I play with a pick, but I've got the whole thing down." So I woodshedded hard, influenced for this type of run-and-gun gigging by DeGrasso: I remembered he had joined Megadeth and nailed eighteen songs in front of five thousand people with no rehearsal. I knew that was how I needed to be now on this Montrose gig, because we were going to show up in Florida, do a sound check, and be onstage a few hours later. I needed to be the guy who turns up and knows his parts. I've been like that ever since, whether it's a church gig or on the last Megadeth album: I show up completely prepared. It was really good for my musicianship.

Just like Jimmy's coming into Megadeth, my audition with Ronnie Montrose was at a sound check, of the first show in Tampa, Florida. We continued to play together for about a year and a half, and they were fun gigs. I'd go to bed after each gig on such a high. His approach was "Play this song just like the recording until the solo, and then I'll see you later. At some point I'll come back around and we'll hook back up again for the main riff or chorus and finish out the song." It was such a cool approach, one that I hadn't taken before, but that I really enjoyed. Jimmy said to me at one point, "I've never heard you play bass like this: you're throwing in runs and licks everywhere!" It was a totally liberating approach for me.

An unusual request came in 2007 by e-mail from rapper Ron Braunstein, whose stage name is Necro. I didn't know anything about rap music or rap-rock, although I was familiar with the Red Hot Chili Peppers and Faith No More. What got me excited about playing with

Necro was that Scott Ian of Anthrax was playing on his album *Death Rap*, so I did it, thinking that, if nothing else, it was a great way for me and Scott to work together.

I'd never played on anything like that before, and I decided not to close my mind to it but to see if I could learn from it. I did it remotely, recording my bass tracks in Pro Tools and e-mailing them over. That same year, I recorded a couple of instructional metal bass DVDs for a company called Rock House Method, who did a lot of work with Peavey. I did one DVD for beginners and the second for advanced level, rather than just one that was all about shredding. Life was suddenly full of exciting, but very different, projects of this kind.

In 2007, I was invited to play the tenth anniversary of the Rock and Roll Fantasy Camp in Las Vegas. It was a big one, with Slash, Vince Neil, Roger Daltrey, and Nicko McBrain, who I persuaded to come out and play at the event. I was pretty good at putting things together with people, and I felt Nicko would be a good addition from the metal world. Plus, he and I had gotten along very well in years past. I was hired as a counselor for the camp. My job was to put together a curriculum for each day, which involved my group of five musician camp attendees learning a song and playing it to a live audience that night, the big finale being a concert on the last night at the Mandalay Bay House of Blues. I loved it. I had real momentum at this point, because everything I did fed into the next project I got involved with. It was a lot of fun. Mark Slaughter, whom I'd known for years and always got on real well with, became a close friend and mentor to me that week.

That led to another gig with the Fantasy Camp, a corporate event out in Hawaii, which was much less enjoyable, because I was really out of my element. Mark Hudson, the TV personality, was the musical director and when we were up on the bandstand, he was calling off all kinds of music. He actually had a good sense of showbiz and knew how to have fun onstage. He was really big on playing songs that got the audience rocking, not just songs the musicians wanted to play. I didn't disagree with him, but these were tunes from another generation. He was calling out songs from Booker T & the MGs, the Beatles, and so on—and some of these were songs that I didn't know. It really taught me that I had to bone up on the music.

At one point during the gig, Bruce Kulick (a fine musician who was in KISS, among other bands) was up there, too, and said to me, "Dude, give me the bass, I'll get us through this" and so I handed my bass to him. I have to be honest here: it was totally humiliating. I was embarrassed. Being the guy from Megadeth gave me zero credibility among these musicians, because they were all older and more experienced than me.

The experience made me realize that since the age of twenty, I'd had a record deal and had performed all original music as a result, the odd exception such as "These Boots Are Made For Walkin'" aside. I hadn't played cover tunes since I was a teenager in Minnesota. Now I needed to broaden my horizons, and it was a real wake-up call. Mark Hudson was on me constantly, like, "Come on, it's the Beatles! You need to learn these tunes! Kid, you gotta get yourself a rock 'n' roll book...."

Kip Winger, who was a good friend of mine, told me not to worry about Mark, but he was right. I needed to step up. I really woodshedded to get through it: I thought, "Let me pretend that Mark Hudson is looking over my shoulder right now," and I really boned up. My goal became to get his approval, and ultimately I achieved that aim and it really broadened my playing. Mark became a real mentor to me on those camps and we became good friends as a result. I guess the lesson there is that you can tuck your tail between your legs and run away, or face the music and see it as an opportunity to grow. Fortunately, I chose the latter.

Glenn Hughes (Black Country Communion, ex-Deep Purple): I met

David in the mid-'90s through mutual friends. I spent
quite a bit of time with him one-on-one in a Rock and
Roll Fantasy Camp U.S. tour in 2008. He really is one of
our industry's good guys. I always love spending time
with David. He introduced me to his lovely daughter at
the 2013 Grammys, and I told her she was a lucky girl to
have such a great dad. Need someone reliable, who will
always show up, rain or shine, with a spring in his step?
That's David Ellefson.

I also played with singer Tim "Ripper" Owens, whom I'd first met in
1998 when Judas Priest were supporting Megadeth in Monterrey and
Mexico City—not the other way around, like it was on *Rust in Peace*
back in 1990 to '91. Tim was Priest's singer at the time, and he seemed
like a nice guy. Now, a few years later, Tim was a solo artist and a good
neighbor in the heavy metal community.

During the winter NAMM show of 2008, Rock House Method
wanted to put together an all-star heavy metal band for a jam at their
annual event, which was at a club in the lobby of the Hilton hotel in
Anaheim, California. So I called Jason Bittner of Shadows Fall, Rob Ar-
nold from Chimaira, and Marc Rizzo from Soulfly to put a lineup together. Jason suggested getting Tim to sing, which is how that

connection came about. We rehearsed some tunes the night before, but Tim couldn't make the rehearsal, so at the show the next day he walked out onstage unrehearsed. We knocked out the tunes, though, and it sounded awesome. It was so good, and I was truly impressed with Tim's ability to walk in and just nail the parts.

The following September, Mark Abbattista, a music business attorney and artist manager friend of mine, called me with an idea. He wanted to put a band together to tour in South America in January 2009. The idea was that famous guys would go down and play songs from the metal genre, in a group he wanted to call Hail! I told him I'd just worked with Ripper at NAMM and that he should be the singer, and Jimmy DeGrasso—who Mark also represented—should play drums. He also suggested Andreas Kisser of Sepultura, who represented the South American thrash contingent. It was a bold idea but one we felt would work with the right list of songs.

In January of 2009 we flew to Santiago, Chile, and put the plan into motion. We had a set list of about twenty songs and, sight unseen for Andreas, we plugged in and tore into "Ace of Spades." It sounded great! It was so cool. We rehearsed for only a couple of days and did a little preview show the night before the tour. The fans absolutely loved it. It rocked my world, playing to the fans in Chile, and it seemed they were happy to see me again, too. The shows were great: there were six of them in five cities across the country, and it was one of the most fun tours I've ever done. We did Hail! tours all around the world after that.

Looking back at all this cool stuff makes me think. I realize now that my early years in Megadeth were not only tough, but they were the ones that would prepare me for the life to follow, too. The eight years away from the band, and the recent years in which I have been a member of Megadeth once more, have been my favorite years since I was eighteen, largely because of the experiences I had from 2002 to 2010, which really changed my life and my music. Who would ever have predicted that?

A THOUGHT

Inspirations

Over and over again, I've been shown that some of the best things that have ever happened to me were never my idea. They come to me in the form of a phone call or an e-mail, or I may simply run into someone out of the blue who asks for my participation in a project. I have to chalk this up to some type of faith that life will provide you with all you need.

I have also learned that when someone asks, the best response is yes. After all, they didn't ask so I would say no. It keeps life fun and improvisational and keeps me on my toes. Isn't that what living is all about?

CHAPTER THIRTEEN

MEGA Life!

> "The thief comes only to steal and kill and destroy: I have come that they may have life, and have it to the full."
>
> —John 10:10

In the meantime, I maintained my sobriety, which remained my number-one priority. While doing so, I encountered other musicians whose paths had also led them into addiction.

Randy Blythe (Lamb of God):

The first time I met David was in Phoenix, when he was working for Peavey. He was backstage and my drummer, Chris Adler, a huge Megadeth fan, introduced me to him. We had a lovely talk. He's a very well-rounded man who takes things as they come. You don't see a lot of anxiety in him, which appeals to me.

I had a long struggle with alcohol. It can be a lonely place trying to stay sober when everyone else around you is partying, so when I want to know how to do something, I look to older, wiser people who have done it before. David is one of those guys. He's been sober a long time, and he's continued to play music. I talked about him with some other sober musicians, and they said, "He's a good guy to talk to. He knows the deal."

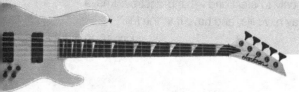

The fundamental question I ask myself is: What makes an addict an addict? What I've discovered is that it's different for everybody. My sponsor Craig S. always said that trying to figure that out is like trying to rearrange deck chairs on the *Titanic*. You're going down, so get the heck off the ship! In other words, rather than throw another rock of crack into the crack pipe and sit and contemplate, get out of the crack house.

It has been written that when a substance goes into an alcoholic's body, something happens that does not happen in a normal person: a phenomenon of craving develops and they're off to the races. After they've gone on a few sprees and possibly been to jail, or gotten divorced, or been made homeless . . . they come to their senses and realize that they have to stop. A normal person would just stop before that point, if it ever got that bad. An alcoholic's mind will justify their behavior because the lure of the bottle is so powerful that they have no defenses against it, and they keep going back to it.

So it's a twofold thing: a physical addiction and a mental urge to return to the substance, sometimes even when the addict is already sober. That is where the recovery process comes in: it's the spiritual medicine that fixes it. That's why you can't just give a pill to an alcoholic and say, "Take this and call me in the morning—everything should be better." That was what I thought rehab was going to be: I thought they would give me the "don't drink" pill and I'd be good to go. But it isn't like that: the spiritual enlightenment and awakening that occurs is sudden for some people.

In Acts 9 of the New Testament, Paul witnesses a white light on the road to Damascus. He hates Christians and he kills them, and suddenly he experiences this light and he is completely transformed and born again in that moment. It's as if the Holy Spirit tapped him and said, "You're done doing that: I need you over on the winning team!" I realized that alcoholics and addicts get tapped, too. This can occur through a "come to Jesus" vision or through a slower, more educational experience—in my case, one that took place over an eighteen-month period, from 1988 to 1990.

I came to believe and then I walked away from my drink and my drugs. I had a week of sobriety, then a month, and then a year. Over time I was transformed. We all need to be transformed in order to defeat our addictions. We learn new disciplines to replace the old ones. It takes work: it's not enough to simply sit at home and say, "Isn't this great? I'm saved! I'm good to go." No. We need prayer and instruction and fellowship. We need all of those things, because they form the process of recovery.

Are we all addicts? Well, my pastor would argue that we're all addicts to sin. Each of us has some form of hang-up in our lives, our cross to bear, if you will. For some it may be greed or lust. For others it's work. Others seek to avoid confrontation. You can fill in your own blank. I agree with my pastor on one level; however, I think that a chemical addiction lies outside that realm, because drugs and alcohol were never meant to be put into our bodies in the first place. We can clearly do without those things.

In my case, my early sponsors approached my behavior not as a sin but as a misalignment of my natural qualities. This misalignment occurs in many instances. For example, money is given to us so that we can provide for our families and be self-sustaining, but used selfishly it leads to greed, which is selfish. Every one of the seven deadly sins is basically a naturally occurring quality in humans that is abused and becomes a sin. Sin can simply be described as something that separates us from our Creator and our fellows. In other words, we play God because we are deluded enough to think that we know better, and that we can handle it on our own.

We all become a product of our environment. Drugs and booze are everywhere when you're in a rock band. Some people have to get off the road and even out of the business entirely to save themselves, because it's an environment that takes them down every time they get into it. My personal experience that I refer back to is the time I got started playing bass when I was eleven years old. Did I do it for sex and drugs? No. I did it for my love of rock 'n' roll. I fell into those other things along the way, and I definitely needed spiritual help to get out of them and remain out of them.

In the Bible, there is also talk of spiritual warfare amongst us. It declares that this war is fought in the heavenly realms and that it is between God and Satan. However, those attacks are made toward us. Whether you subscribe to that belief or not, it certainly explains a lot of otherwise unexplainable stuff. In Ephesians 6 it says that we should put on the full armor of the Lord so that we will be protected. For me, that is the right approach. I get up each morning and put on the protection of the Lord, because I know from personal experience that the enemy is out there waiting.

When I'm physically fit, I'm healthy: when I'm spiritually fit, I'm healthy. If I fall short in either of those things, it's easy to get off track. I have a responsibility to stay fit on both levels, so I'm covered. Addiction is selfish: it's all about wanting to feel good right now, so you say, "Hand me the joint," to get immediate gratification. Recovery is all about letting that process do for you slowly what the dope does quickly. More than that, it is about serving others, so as much as I might want to do something to feel good right now, my ultimate responsibility now is first and foremost to my sobriety, which is obedience to the Creator. This aligns the will to do His bidding on this planet. From there, we can serve our other purposes. I do my best to align them as God, family, work. Those are the priorities I've learned work best.

For me, prayer is huge. It is the one method of spiritual communication I've seen work wonders in my life. So I pray every day, wherever I am in the world. In the beginning, I didn't know who or what I was praying to, but things started to happen. Skeptical though I was, the evidence ruled against my doubts.

Part of any spiritual awakening is the journey itself. That journey usually includes seeking out fellowship with like-minded believers. This is what led me back to the doors of the church, if for no other reason than for my family to have a home with God.

These days, I find that modern church culture is fantastic. It is much different from what it was when I was growing up. Nowadays it is tied in with social media and with cool, uplifting rock music. For people of my age it needed to make that shift to remain relevant. In fact, that musical shift inside the church came from people of my age, many of whom are musicians who have toured and played out, gotten married, grown up, and realized that at some point, they can bring their guitar or bass into church and continue to rock out for a different cause. Even better, in church you don't have hecklers, and you can bring your wife and kids, because no one's drinking beer, throwing up, and spewing vulgarities at you. It has really expanded in that direction.

I have become good friends with a number of Christian musicians, one of whom is Jesse Reeves, who plays bass with the singer-songwriter Chris Tomlin.

Jesse Reeves (bassist, Chris Tomlin's band): I first met David in the mid-2000s at a Christian music summit in Seattle. The worship leader pointed him out to me and told me his name was David. I looked over at him and said, "Is that David Ellefson from Megadeth?" He was like, "You know who he is?" and I said, "Man, I grew up listening to him!"

The Bible tells us to be a light in a lost world, and the danger of that is that you have to be in that lost world. You have to immerse yourself in it. Sadly, more times than not, the world brings the Christian down, instead of letting the Christian raise up the world, and what I've come to appreciate about Ellefson is that he is really trying to make a difference in the world. I have nothing but respect for him.

Here's a quick footnote from history which I find fascinating. In 1517, the German theologian Martin Luther challenged the political agenda of the Catholic priesthood, which taught at the time that believers could buy their way into heaven. Luther went back to Scripture, read it, and declared that the church was doing it all wrong. They were not following what Jesus said. Instead, they were really using it for their own political and personal gain.

That was the start of the Reformation, the Protestant movement, and the origins of the Lutheran Church. This process extended when people such as my ancestors in the Ellefson family began to migrate en masse from northern Europe to North America in the seventeenth century. They brought their religion with them, in much the same way that Irish and Italian immigrants brought Catholicism with them.

Speaking of this development, there is a board of elders at our church, and at one point they wanted to elect me to be an elder. At that time I couldn't do it because I was traveling so much. A few years later, they asked me again and I was able to say yes. I was brought in as an elder for a two-year term. I was initially reluctant because I didn't know what it entailed, although they turned out to be a pretty relaxed bunch of guys. In fact, one of the first meetings took place at a Mexican restaurant and these guys put away quite a bit of beer. It was cool, though: these people weren't alcoholics and they were perfectly entitled to a beer with their chips if they wanted one.

I believe, as Luther did, that the Bible speaks the truth, and that is why I was honored in 2006 when Pastor Jon Bjorgaard of the Shepherd of the Desert Lutheran Church and School asked me to lead a new contemporary worship group. He knew about my history in the rock world and also about my life in the Christian community, and he suggested the name MEGA Life!, an obvious play on my former band name as well as the basis in scripture of John 10:10.

Pastor Jon Bjorgaard (Shepherd of the Desert Lutheran Church, Scottsdale, Arizona): David and I began

MEGA Life! as a Sunday-evening service. As it grew, after a year and a half or so, we moved it to Sunday morning. He has a real passion for helping people who are struggling with addiction and he is very involved in mentoring and sponsoring people. The area of ministry that we're looking for him to work in is community outreach, where we connect the church with the outside world. It's been really interesting to watch David travel the world with his band and sponsor people while he's away.

David is a great guy: he's one of the most genuine people you could ever meet. Sometimes I forget about his celebrity status: we'll go out to lunch, and people will walk up to the table and ask for his autograph. Ours is a pretty conservative denomination, and he's not really from the typical mold—which is a good thing, in my opinion, because that will help us to reach out to people who we wouldn't normally reach. He has a wonderful family, too: his wife and kids are fantastic.

I didn't grow up listening to Megadeth: I was more into mainstream groups like Foreigner. But I've become a Megadeth fan through David: I really like some of their music. The vast majority of the congregation are very

supportive of the fact that he plays in the band. It's a great thing for our church. He brings in a new perspective.

I was honored, of course, although I was a little worried that Megadeth fans would consider it a bit dorky that I had gone from playing bass in stadiums to playing bass in church. My human pride kicked in a little there, I suppose, but I realized that anyone who would want me to stay in the same spiritual place of addiction that I had previously occupied is not someone whose approval I needed anyway. That was a revelation to me, and it took a long time for me to get there.

I started the new MEGA Life! group, holding auditions for musicians. On the first day of auditions, Julie and my kids came rushing into the church and told me that my mother had suffered a severe stroke back in Minnesota. She was only seventy-two years old. She had survived it, but she was at the hospital back in Sioux Falls, South Dakota. I immediately booked a flight and flew up to see her. My mother had been somewhat of a shining star in VH1's *Behind the Music* special on Megadeth for her sweet candor. When she had her stroke, a friend put the word out to the metal community, and we were showered with prayers and thoughtful words to her from the fans. It was truly a touching moment. Within a week, she'd taken up residence in the same nursing home where she had worked for the twenty years since I'd left home, back in Jackson, Minnesota.

My pastor told me when I came back to Arizona that when the Lord decides to do something like the MEGA Life! project, Satan tries his hardest to distract leaders away from him. Not that my mother's stroke was an act of Satan, but rather that it could be a distraction for me to not pursue the worship service. That was the first time I really connected the personal issues of spiritual warfare that I mentioned earlier.

As the MEGA Life! leader, I was on the church staff for about three years, and I learned many things. I realized that to people who don't go to church, it can seem from the outside like a bunch of self-righteous, flawless people who run the place. Well, I'm here to tell you something: it isn't just the holy who go to church! All of us have earned our place there, including the sickest of the sick. Ironically, as a supposed rock star and heavy metal guy, I was able to enter the church with a fairly practical approach to it, not trying to be grandiose and using it as a platform for my own notoriety. My approach was much more street level.

The benefits of attending church are many. When I was growing up, my life was a lot more stable and I felt a lot less fear. I felt better about myself and my place in the world as a regular churchgoer. That feeling of safety has come back to me in my adult life from my church attendance. I didn't realize this a few years ago, though. My feelings about church were that it was culturally irrelevant, that it was dated, and that it was for my parents' generation, not mine. Then, like I said, the church reinvented itself, and that was something that I wanted to continue with MEGA Life!

I quickly wrote a lot of songs for the worship group when I was the leader. If we needed a communion song, or a song for benediction, I'd write it. Essentially a service will be comprised of three songs plus a sermon and shared testimony. For two years MEGA Life! was an evening service, and after that it became a morning event.

After all of these transitions I was finally in a good place. I had graduated college; I had been in my own bands; I'd worked for Peavey; and I was involved in worship ministry at church. I had a pretty well-rounded life with a lot of stability. I thrived in these aspects of my life.

Rather than feeling like a boat bobbing up and down on the ocean, I now felt like a pontoon with stabilizers on all sides.

A THOUGHT

The Bass Guitar—and How to Play It

To me, playing any instrument well requires that you do it often. Practicing at home is good, but there's nothing like being in a band room or on a stage with other musicians regularly. It's the thing that really tightens you up as a player. As far as I'm concerned, it's not about being the flashiest bassist, but rather about being consistently solid and stable in the band, whatever style you play.

The greatest bass player who ever lived? I'm not sure there is a "greatest" anything or anyone, because everyone brings something unique to the table with their style of playing. Some of the more special ones to me are Steve Harris, Geddy Lee, and Bob Daisley, who played in Rainbow and on the early Ozzy records. Those guys had very melodic and interesting lines and they are also great songwriters, which probably has a lot to do with why their bass lines are so prominent in their music. They are artists as well as bassists, and I've learned a lot from that approach in my own career.

We have so many generations of great music behind us now that there are a lot of genres, players, and influences to draw from. Whatever style you like to play, make sure you do your homework and learn the basics, too. Learn things like the blues and classic rock songs; learn some Beatles, Zeppelin, and country; and study the basics of jazz. In fact, once you learn Jazz 101 you will essentially have the basics to play with anyone, anywhere, and in any key.

It's important to dumb it down and play some punk rock, so you can learn how to have some raw emotion in your music, too. Being refined is great, but most music I've ever played sounds best when it has some kicking energy to it and is not just played perfectly all the time. I think there's something we can all learn from the three-chord bands like the Clash, the Sex Pistols, the Ramones, and, more recently, Green Day and Nirvana. That music is all about spirit, even though it may be lacking in some refinement. Also, learn to play by ear, because that can become your most valuable asset on any bandstand anywhere. Most bands don't have sheet music, so don't get too used to reading maps when you should be looking at the road signs anyway. Oh, and don't snub the pick!

A lot of modern metal is tuned way down to B and even low A. Some of that stuff can be played on a four-string that is strung B, E, A, D, basically eliminating the high-G string. But since I learned how to play bass more formally, not knowing where the notes are in dropped tunings drives me crazy. I would rather grab a five-string and have all those notes available to me in a manner that is musically correct, even if I have to tune it down a whole step for a low A tuning. It keeps me from having to widen the nut space on the low strings, too. Plus, over- all there is more wood in the body and neck of a five-string bass, and sometimes a longer scale length, which makes it better for reproducing the lower tunings.

CHAPTER FOURTEEN

Coming Full Circle

"Somewhere early in my life the Holy Trinity went from Father, Son, and Holy Ghost to sex, drugs, and rock 'n' roll. Even stranger is that it all came full circle and restored itself to its natural order."

—David Ellefson

Things continued to move forward on the musical front. In 2009 I played bass for Tim "Ripper" Owens on a short European tour, which he was doing to support his solo album at the time. Heavy metal singer Ronnie James Dio's wife and manager, Wendy Dio, was managing Tim, so she put us on several dates with Ronnie's band Heaven and Hell and gave us an opening slot on the main stage of the Download Festival. I ran into our former booking agent John Jackson backstage and we embraced, having not seen each other for several years. I had apologized back in 1994 for putting him in a bad position after my meltdown at Donington in 1988, and we became good friends after that. That can happen when you acknowledge your shortcomings to people.

John told me that he was launching a new festival called Sonisphere, and also that he was thinking about doing a festival of the "Big Four" thrash bands—Metallica, Slayer, Megadeth, and Anthrax—in 2010. What's funny is that I was one of the few musicians who knew about the Big Four dates, and yet I wasn't in any of the bands at that time.

That said, hints that things might be about to change in that area were making themselves felt. In the early summer of 2009, my family rented a house up in the mountains to get away from the heat in Scottsdale, and Dave started reaching out to me again by phone. We hadn't met since we'd failed to make the Nashville thing work, and now here we were trying to heal some wounds. Hooking up with Megadeth was beginning to look like it could be a lot of fun again.

I played an F5 show in the middle of July, the same weekend as NAMM's summer show in Nashville. We flew into Nashville to play the show, and as soon as I landed, I received a text from Dave asking where I was. I thought he might be in town doing something with Dean Guitars, whose instruments he endorses, so I reached back to him. He told me that he was at home in San Diego but wanted to know if I wanted to fill in on something that was coming up.

After F5's sound check, he and I got on the phone: it was the first time we had talked in three years. It was a very positive conversation, and I thought the next step should be that we would hang out together. It was only a seventy-five-minute flight from Phoenix to San Diego, so a few days later I flew out to see him for an afternoon, just to see if we could be buddies again. He picked me up at the airport and we hung out at his new studio and his home. I flew home again and felt really good about things.

Dave was very excited, too, and wanted to announce that I was back in the band. With things moving quickly at this point, he and his manager wanted to call me to discuss money. I replied that money had been such a problem between us in the past that I would rather they spoke to my attorney, who would negotiate the deal on my behalf. He knew I wanted to do it and wasn't going to get in my way, so I took my hands off the wheel and redirected them to him.

Predictably, everything went south from there, and the reunion didn't happen that time. I'd gone to see Judas Priest play in Phoenix that night. They were playing the whole of their *British Steel* album, and I remember thinking how cool it would be if Megadeth ever did the same thing. I was down there, hanging with the Judas Priest guys, having some laughs and catching up on old times, and later that night I checked my BlackBerry—and there was an e-mail from Dave saying that my attorney had asked for too much money. It had been so close to, and yet so far away from, working out.

But Megadeth and I weren't done yet, not by a long shot, owing to a set of circumstances that were so fortuitous I have to regard them as a collective act of God. In January 2010, I was back at the NAMM show yet again in Anaheim, California, doing my job at the Peavey booth. On the Friday night of the show, Dave was going to play at Dean Guitars' party at the Grove in Anaheim. I was out to dinner with one of the guys from Hartke, who was talking to me about some endorsement stuff. After dinner I checked my BlackBerry and there was a text from Willie Gee, Dave's guitar tech. It read, "Mr. Ellefson, Willie Gee here. Just wondering if you might be available to jump up and play a song with Dave at the Grove?"

I replied that I had a bass with me and that I would be available to play, and that he should just let me know. Later he texted back to say that Megadeth's current bassist James LoMenzo was going to play instead, and thanked me. I said that it was no problem and that he should tell Dave that I had his back either way, which he apparently communicated to Dave.

The next day, Shawn Drover, the drummer of Megadeth, walked over to the Peavey booth and said hello. I liked Shawn a lot. I'd spoken to him on the phone in the summer of 2009 when Dave and I had talked about rejoining the band. He's a solid man on his own two feet and he's a gentleman. He has wisdom and clarity, and he totally understands his role and position in the band without assuming or presuming anything. In short, he's a real musician I knew I'd like to be in a band with.

I said, "It's too bad I didn't get to play with you last night. Dave and I back together onstage would have been a great news story." He said, "I know—it would have been great!" I added that if things didn't work out with James LoMenzo, he should give me a call, and he nodded with an amused smile. We shook hands and I forgot all about it.

However, Shawn is a Megadeth fan to the core, and he knew that they had to get me back in the band.

Shawn Drover (drummer, Megadeth): I've been a fan of Megadeth since day one. I still remember hearing songs from *Killing Is My Business* . . . on a metal show on the radio in Montreal, where I grew up. I joined the band in late 2004, when Dave re-formed the band. In early 2010, we were getting ready to record the song "Sudden Death" for a *Guitar Hero* game. Somewhere in the middle of it Dave Mustaine informed me that we needed to get another bass player. The fans had seen numerous lineups come and go over the years, and they were really embracing James LoMenzo at that point—for good reason, as he is a great bass player and a great guy. Within a couple of minutes of this conversation, I thought to myself, "I wonder if I can get in touch with David Ellefson? What better person to have on board?"

Two pivotal announcements were made at this time, both of which made a profound impact on me. One was regarding John Jackson's original plan, which had come to fruition. As he had suggested, the Big Four of thrash metal announced European festival dates together. This was a historic gathering by anybody's standards, and I wanted to be there. Secondly, Megadeth was going to play the *Rust in Peace* album in its entirety on a U.S. tour in March, to celebrate its twentieth anniversary.

We were in New York with Hail!, about to play two shows in the area with ex–Dream Theater drummer Mike Portnoy. We were on our way to do Eddie Trunk's radio show when I received the press release about the Rust in Peace tour coming up a month later. I thought, "Man, I need to be there for this!" I knew all the songs and I knew it was the right thing to do for our legacy, if the door was in any way still open for me to join in. Portnoy was saying, "You should be there for that. It's not right that you're not." I then had to go on Eddie Trunk's show and do the interview, even though I felt like I'd been kicked in the gut when I saw that press release on my phone.

Shawn Drover (drummer, Megadeth): At the time, the Rust in Peace tour was only for America: of course, it turned into a full-blown world tour, but at the time, it was just a one-month run and we would then have resumed touring for our most recent album. So I wondered if David would be up for coming in and helping us out, as we were about to lose our bass player. Dave's guitar tech Willie Gee had David's cell phone number and so he called him.

Then, on February 2, which is my son Roman's birthday, I was at home having dinner with my family. Shortly after, I walked into my office and I happened to see my BlackBerry blinking. It was another message from Willie Gee, asking me to call him. I said to Julie, "Here we go again!" and made the call. I talked to Shawn, who told me that James LoMenzo would be leaving the band. He and I corresponded by text over the next couple of days. It was such a bizarre and immediate thing to happen, because I was sitting in a pastors' conference in Phoenix and I got a text from him saying, "Dude. If there was ever a time for you to reach out to Dave, it is right now!"

Notice the irony of this: I'm sitting in a church conference (my future) while Megadeth (my past) is reaching out to me. But as much as I loved my volunteering in the church, I knew that if I was ever going to kick the tires of Megadeth and drive it around the block to see if it was still a good ride, this was the time to do it. I could do everything else another time: they would always be there for me, while Megadeth might not. I also knew that tickets for the Rust in Peace tour were on sale, so I told them that I was both available and interested.

Shawn Drover (drummer, Megadeth): I told him that we had a situation, that we were about to go and do this Rust in Peace tour and that we had a spot for a bass player. I told him that if he even had an inkling of interest, I needed to hear it right then: not next week, but right then. I was calling him out of the blue, so he was probably thinking, "What the hell is going on here?" but I must have sparked his interest. I told Dave Mustaine, who agreed to a conference call

with the three of us. I stayed on the line for ten minutes but I could tell they needed to talk, so I put the phone down and they had a conversation.

I called Dave at the studio, where he was recording, and he and I and Shawn got on the phone. Dave was real clear about what was on the table. He said, "This is the amount of money I can pay you." If I'm being completely honest, at that point I didn't care about the money. I was like, "Let's just go do this, I want to be part of this again." That was on February 4, 2010.

I drove over to the band's studio north of San Diego the next day with a couple of basses in my car. Fortunately I'd kept my chops up and retained my knowledge of the Megadeth catalog over the years. People were always asking me at bass clinics about Megadeth songs, and it was a matter of personal and professional pride to me that I could always pull out a certain lick if they wanted to hear it. So I went over and we rehearsed.

Shawn Drover (drummer, Megadeth): The next day David was on his way over to see us. To witness the two Daves playing together was just awesome. You could tell that it was comfortable for them to play together again, like putting on some old shoes. As a drummer, it was very easy for me to lock in with Ellefson's bass playing. No disrespect to his successors, who were excellent bass players, but it was great to form a rhythm section with the guy who laid down those bass parts in the first place. From the point of view of a fan, and in the best possible interests of the band, I just had to get them back together—and I pulled it off!

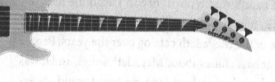

The first song we played was "Symphony of Destruction," which sounded great. We looked at each other and we knew right away it was going to work. After that we went out to dinner, and Dave told me that he was impressed with the way I looked and played. He said, "You've got the life that I've always wanted." Just for him to say that was enough. We hugged and he said, "Are we going to do this?" and I nervously said yes. He went home thrilled, and I thought to myself, "What did I just commit to?"

I have a tendency to do this: it's a shortcoming of mine. My initial reaction was "Never mind the money: let's just do it!" but then my head kicked in and I started worrying. But once your head starts getting involved, that's your ego getting in the way. Don't listen to it, although I did on this occasion. I called Dave and told him that I was worried about letting go of the Peavey gig and all the things I had in my life, and he was devastated—but he reassured me, and I was in.

There's a saying that goes "You will keep being presented with a lesson until you finally learn that lesson," and this was my lesson. To finally jump in and stop trying to control the outcome, to have faith that it will all work out as it should. Over the weekend I played on the new Megadeth track "Sudden Death," which was being used on the *Guitar Hero* computer game. But I was still worried all that weekend, and on Monday morning I had a long conversation with Dave where I laid all my fears on the table. I told him that we'd been through a lot together. He told me, "Why don't we take it one day at a time?" and quoted Scripture, reminding me that the Israelites took forty years to make a journey that should have taken eleven days. How long were we going to wander around like that, he asked? We would never know until we tried it. Sometimes Dave's wisdom is pretty simple, and this time I heard it.

I got home and handed the phone to Julie, who talked to Dave and asked about his wife, Pam, and their children, and they had some laughs together. After that, Julie and I talked, and she said, "You need to do this. You haven't been really happy since you left the band, and Dave is really asking you to come back. Do it because you're his friend. Don't even do it as the bass player for Megadeth: just do it as a friend. If it doesn't work, at least you two will walk away as friends."

As it happened, Peavey were making cutbacks at the time, and after seven years with them, my job went away—just as I was rejoining the band. If that isn't a sign of a higher power at work, I don't know what is. I was grateful to them for my job there. I got to study business and apply those principles in the real world at the same time. It was a great eight-year period of my life that was about to transition once more.

Initially I signed up for the one-month Rust in Peace U.S. tour. Shawn told me, "Come on, it's just a month," probably knowing full well that a month would turn into a permanent commitment. And I'm glad he did it, because when I rejoined Megadeth in February 2010, I really felt that a new season of my life had begun. I handed the reins of MEGA Life! to a good friend, Ray Berry, and when I'm in town share my testimony there about once a year. I also play bass in the services when the schedule allows, and my wife and kids have been able to let go of their service commitments and attend with other regular church-goers. It's really lovely.

Meanwhile, I've been able to transition into other areas of service in the church community. I'm now the director of community out-reach, and I've been able to put other alcohol and drug recovery–based courses in place, too. Over the years I've learned that a spirit of rotation is good for us when doing volunteer work. It keeps us from trying to take ego-based ownership of things, and it allows for other people to be able to step up and serve with their talents, too.

The Rust in Peace tour was an incredible high for us. We played Latin America and then did a full seven-week tour of Europe. From there we rolled right into the Big Four dates. One of the coolest things was that Metallica called a band dinner, the night before the first show in Warsaw, for the band members only, with no managers or other as-sociates. Robert Trujillo was the greeter at the front door of the restau-rant and as soon as we walked in, Kirk Hammett and Dave started chatting. It was a great opportunity just to break bread with each other before the shows actually started. We did the hang before we actually played any music.

James Hetfield and I had a chance to connect for the first time. As much as our two bands have been around each other over the years, it was great to rekindle my friendship with those guys. The next day at the first show, James was standing outside the dressing rooms, cheering everybody on and shouting, "Have a great show!" A band that big doesn't have to do that: they could just as easily retreat to their dressing rooms and after the show hop on a Learjet and be out of there. But that wasn't Metallica's style. It was genuinely like we were one big family. We weren't going back in time to re-create thrash metal. Instead, we were unifying thrash metal in one huge, connected front, truly for the first time ever.

After that European stint came the American Carnage tour, which was interesting because these were rescheduled dates that had been supposed to happen back in January. Slayer's singer, Tom Araya, had needed neck surgery and the dates were postponed. In a way, his surgery had opened the door for me to come back to the band because of schedule changes. I just knew that all these things pointed toward my return to Megadeth.

It reminds me of the old story: A Christian guy dies in a flood and goes to heaven, and he says to God, "Why did you let me die? Why did you do this to me?" and God says to him, "When your neighbor told you to evacuate the building, and you said no, because you thought God would save you. That was me. Then, when your friend came past in a boat and offered you a lift to safety, but you said no because God would save you, that was me, too. And then, when the helicopter came down to pick you up from the roof of the building, and you said no yet again because you knew that God would save you, that was me, coming to get you out of the mess you were in!"

The opportunity to rejoin Megadeth this time was like that helicopter: it was as if God was saying to me, "You need to get back there now." When James LoMenzo left the band, there was really only one bass player who could take his place. It all lined up.

Everything was really going well. Dave and I spent a lot of time together reading scripture, and the synergy was back between us. He and I both had the exact same study Bible. You think that's a coincidence? Well, there's a saying that there are no coincidences in God's world, because He has orchestrated it all. The Book of Proverbs has thirty-one proverbs in it, one for every day of the month, so if in doubt, right before we went onstage, if we had a bit of time backstage, or when we were grabbing a coffee in the lobby when we woke up, we would kick back and soak up the Bible. That was our personal connection. The more time we spent with the Bible, the closer we got and the better the band sounded. It was a form of faith development, and it just goes to show that when you put first things first, all the rest will handle itself.

It was like putting together a jigsaw puzzle: you can spend so much time looking for one particular piece, and when you go away to answer the phone, you come back and that piece has been lying in front of you the whole time. That's how I see my experience. Because Dave and I were so driven in the early days and so focused on work, we missed out on our faith development, which was always right in front of us. The days that we do that together are still my favorite days on the bus. Shawn likes it because he sees that it joins us and brings us closer together, and so he takes part, too: that's what I love about him, that he's a very pragmatic, calming kind of person.

In the old days we used to get together with straws and lines of drugs on the table: that was our connection back then. That obviously didn't work very well, which I think is an important point. People always want to get together, whether it's over music or a couple of drinks or whatever, but anything that is derived of man will ultimately fall short and divide you.

Now we've found a connection that is bigger than all of us, and its only common goal is loving, serving, and connecting each other. There is no downside to helping others, and on my return to Megadeth that was what we tapped into. I've learned that faith is a daily discipline, every day of the week: in fact, some of our crew started good-naturedly calling me "Pastor Dave" as a result. I had come back with a fresh perspective, to find that Dave and I were seeking to follow our faith walk together. It was as if both of us had been holding the key, but until 2010 we'd never put it in the lock and opened the door.

Fred Kowalo (guitar and bass tech, Megadeth): When David rejoined the band, James LoMenzo told me, "Ellefson's a great guy. You'll love working with him." He was right. You hang around with some guys on the road, and they start wearing you down. With Ellefson, that's not the case. He saw me one day when I was really down and depressed because I'd received bad news from home. He pulled me aside and talked to me. It was Pastor David coming out there. We sat down and talked and we prayed a little bit, and everything turned around. Touring is a hard life, it's really tough, and if you have a guy like Ellefson around who can pick you up and keep you focused, that's a great thing. It's common to have guys say to you on the road, "Hey, let's go party," but not at all common to have someone say to you, "Do you need somebody to talk to, or be there for you?" Also, Ellefson doesn't preach or push religion on you. He doesn't say, "God's looking down on you and he wouldn't approve of what you're doing." He says, "You're human. If my words can help you get through this, then that's great." That's what a good pastor does. He wants to help. That's the great thing about the guy.

A THOUGHT

Faith—and How It Changes You

Life can be funny. It was never my goal to end up back in the church, especially once I got rolling in rock 'n' roll and on my way as a young man in the world. In fact, you could say that once I started rockin', on the church door I would not be knockin'.

However, having faith has a way of changing a person. Experiencing faith as an adult is much different than as a child. What I found was that blending my gifts of music and faith wasn't as much of a stretch as I had previously thought. The truth is, if God is the source of our talents, then I guess He can make even the strangest things happen when used for His glory.

CHAPTER FIFTEEN

Back to the Start

"Carry the Gospel with you wherever you go. Sometimes
you may even have to use words."

—St. Francis

Megadeth was on fire, so we decided to carry on playing *Rust in Peace* when the American Carnage tour began. Slayer and Megadeth together was a great bill. We'd played together as far back as 1985. We're very different musically, but we come from the same genre and we represent the same culture and lifestyle. There were no hostilities between the bands anymore.

We were all playing at our very best. *Endgame,* Megadeth's most recent album, was excellent; the fans had received it really well, and the *Rust in Peace* album still cast a long shadow. We had now become almost a legacy classic metal band, whose history was a big reason why fans would come out to see us. This is a much better position to be in than to record a new album and have the ensuing tour dates stand or fall on whether that album has legs or not. Our legacy was strong now.

We had a lot of creative think-tank sessions, which I call "Starbucks sessions," because the band members would get up in the morning, arrange to meet for coffee, and have a discussion. It's funny that we're such early birds, given that we're a metal band . . . but it's natural. I've done yoga, and I've learned that your body wants to follow the natural rhythms of daylight—as long as you're sober and not staying up all night partying, of course.

The next item on the agenda was the Jägermeister Music Tour, which was essentially Clash of the Titans Part Two, as it featured us, Slayer, and Anthrax (although because the movie remake of *Clash of the Titans* had just been released, we couldn't use that name). I'd done a lot of work with the people at Jägermeister when I was at Peavey. We did a lot of great things together with F5 and Temple of Brutality. The relationship was fantastic and they were stoked about me being back in Megadeth.

Is there a conflict for me, as a sober man, to be working with a company that produces alcoholic drinks? No. One of the things I learned in recovery is that we should not look down our nose at the drinks industry as an institution. I sometimes find that religion takes that attitude: the Bible doesn't tell you not to drink, but it does tell you not to participate in drunkenness. I personally don't take any alcohol into my body because it sets a particular reaction in motion, but I know plenty of people who can drink socially and for whom it's not an issue.

The highlight of that tour was playing at the Gibson Amphitheatre at Universal City. Kerry King hadn't been able to join us in the encore jam at the Big Four show in Sofia, Bulgaria, because he had been called to approve some video footage of Slayer while it was going on, so we invited him to come up and play "Rattlehead" with us onstage. He'd been the very first performing guitarist in Megadeth apart from Dave, so it was a great opportunity to capture the moment. It was cool to have Kerry up there.

I happened to be on the cover of *Bass Player* magazine at that time, which was a huge thing for me. I was so thrilled when they called me about that. They told me that it was high time I was on their cover, as I'd done a lot of writing for them over the years and never been on there. It was the same month as the magazine's Bass Player Live event, too, where I also played, so I was completely thrilled. That was definitely a high point in my career, and even more so because it wasn't simply part of the regular press for a Megadeth album.

We went to Australia in December. That whole year was such a great ride, playing for people all around the world. It was good to be back. Fans saw that there was a genuine camaraderie onstage, the band sounded great, and obviously no one was complaining that we were playing *Rust in Peace* all the way through.

In January 2011, I inked a deal with Jackson Guitars for a signature bass, which you can see at the bottom of this page. My relationship with them is a good one, because, having worked with endorsing artists at Peavey for so long, I can walk into the office and communicate with them on a business level as well as be the famous guy who endorses their instrument. I know the numbers and I know how the machine works, and their office is only fifteen minutes away from my house in Scottsdale, so it's very cool.

Since then I've often performed at bass clinics for Jackson and Hartke, my signature amp manufacturers. I did many of these events in tandem with my friend Frank Bello, the bass player in Anthrax.

Frank Bello (Anthrax): David Ellefson is not only a great bass player and songwriter, he is my friend. He is one of the good guys in music and has always been a great source of knowledge about this business for me. We've done a lot of touring together throughout the years, and Dave has always been and still is that good guy.

NAMM in 2011 was amazing. It was great to be there as a bass player, back with my home band, performing for my peers, which we did at Dean Guitars' Friday-night show at the Grove venue, close by the Anaheim Convention Center.

After NAMM, we went into the songwriting and then the recording sessions for the next Megadeth album, *Thirteen*, which was probably the most fun album I've ever recorded with the band. Within a week I had all of my bass lines for its thirteen songs done and in the can. We brought back "New World Order," which was an old track which we'd demoed in the fall of 1991 in the *Countdown to Extinction* sessions.

Within a ten-week period or so, between the Indio Big Four date and the next Big Four show in Germany, we wrote and recorded the record. We'd never named an album after a number before, and thirteen is a cool, spooky number, so there were a lot of firsts there, among them the fact that it was my first full-length album since I'd rejoined the band.

We played more Big Four shows in Europe in summer 2011 and then joined the Rockstar Energy Drink Mayhem tour in America. Then there was the Big Four show at Yankee Stadium in New York, which looks to have been the last of those shows for now. It was wonderful. I was really happy for the Anthrax guys: it was right in their backyard, after all, with them being the New York champions of the Big Four. It was the final flag in the ground, ending on U.S. shores, where all of the Big Four are from, which had huge significance. It was also bicoastal, because we'd played one in California, too: the two shows on the West and East Coasts represented the origins of the four bands really well.

We released *Thirteen* on November 1, and we played the Jimmy Kimmel show the night before, dressed in Halloween costumes. I was the Wolfman, Dave was Frankenstein, guitarist Chris Broderick was the Phantom of the Opera, and Shawn was Dracula. A couple of days later we flew down to South America to kick off the Thirteen tour and carried on playing live dates all the way through until December 8, 2012. The back end of the tour essentially turned into the *Countdown to Extinction* twentieth-anniversary tour. It was great to celebrate our legacy with these anniversaries as well as create new music.

I looked back and realized that we had pretty much done three years of nonstop touring since I rejoined the band in early 2010. I needed some relaxation time, as everybody in the band did, before we began recording the next Megadeth album, *Super Collider*.

Chris Broderick (guitarist, Megadeth): I love getting together with David because he still has the enthusiasm for music that a young person has. We'll sit down and work on some chord sequences and turnarounds and improvise. When we're working on songs, he'll have suggestions for me and vice versa. It's very cool. He has such a solid, tight rhythm and timing, and he plays right in the pocket with the drums. His picking is right on the money and he knows a lot about harmony, too, so he crafts some great bass lines. You can sense somebody's experience by how quickly they adjust to a new idea or a new environment, and David does that seamlessly, right off the bat. He's a true musician, whether he's playing in Megadeth, or with his worship band, or just picking up an acoustic guitar and playing.

It's been a three-year victory lap for us, and now my kids are three years older. They're really growing up. It's been so rewarding to see Athena take an interest in music: she's artistic and passionate and rapidly becoming the wonderful guitar player and pianist of the Ellefson household. I've also seen my son pursue his interests and become focused on languages, engineering, and sports trivia. To see them become interested in creative arts is a huge thing for me as a father: the cycle feels complete.

When Roman was a baby, he hated it whenever I left to go on tour. He didn't know where I was going; he just knew I was leaving, and he hated it. He was fifteen when I rejoined Megadeth and it was completely different this time. When the press release went out, he immediately received tons of texts and instant messages from his friends saying, "I can't believe your dad's back in Megadeth!" and this time, it was a good thing. It was a big change for him and Athena, of course, although I'm not away for long, extended tours anymore, and we talk via Skype every day.

I still love playing metal, but my least favorite part of the touring experience at this point is the travel. Time zones still create problems for me. My main focus is that ninety minutes to two hours onstage at around eight in the evening, with the gym visit and phone calls in the daytime. Tours these days are better if they last over three weeks, even though that is a long time away from home, simply because you need at least two weeks for your body to get used to that daily routine.

For thirty-five years I've stood in the rifleman's position with my hip twisted and my left arm out, playing a fifteen-pound bass guitar hanging from my shoulder. I've got a chronic chiropractor's issue, which I have to deal with out on tour: my lower left sacrum goes out, and that affects the whole left side of my spine and the vertebrae in my neck, and that can make you sick. Dave, with his martial arts training, can give me a pretty good adjustment: he can twist my lower back so it pops back into place. Most people can't bear to watch, because it looks so painful, but it actually brings great relief. That's my only significant health issue, though.

When traveling I usually only suffer from respiratory issues like bronchitis and sinus stuff: I've been blessed with a strong stomach, and I don't get too ill with food. Nothing is worse than playing onstage with a fever, because just touching your guitar strings hurts and the kick drums thunder through your head, so I normally travel with antibiotics in order to get through it quickly. The feeling is not unlike detoxing from heroin, so getting ill onstage is more or less the only time I ever think of that drug anymore. I don't take any pain relief, either: while my addiction may not be my fault, my recovery is definitely my responsibility, and these days doctors dispense drugs like they're candy—so I have to be vigilant.

My faith walk continues and progresses. I now study in a Senior Mentoring Program, or SMP, for members of a congregation who wish to become ordained. It is run by the Lutheran Church—Missouri Synod seminary in St. Louis, Missouri, which offers online studies. My pastor suggested that I would be a good candidate for it, and so I now spend a week each year on campus in addition to pursuing my online studies. It's something I'm passionate about.

To be accepted into the course was a real miracle: to be saved from heroin addiction, to be rewarded with success, and then to be pulled into church work and still be allowed to sharpen myself with spiritual knowledge is an incredible series of gifts, and an amazing journey. It was interesting, because one or two of my fellow worshippers questioned the fact that a guy in a band called Megadeth could really be studying on this course. I keep my lifestyle clean with even more diligence as a result, especially as I'm now technically Vicar Ellefson, essentially a pastor in training.

As I write this, I'm on a one-year sabbatical to allow myself the necessary time to go through another album and tour cycle. The studies were really enjoyable, although one particular challenge was preparing for stage warm-ups while having my laptop on backstage and keeping an eye on the Tuesday-evening seminary chats that are part of the course. Time zones make that a bit more difficult, too. I will complete the remaining three years: in fact, by the time you read this I will probably have resumed them.

Pastor Jon was a little sad that I had to unplug from my worship leader role with MEGA Life!, but he was excited about me getting more involved in church work. He also told me that my son, Roman, is one of the very few kids he's met who has the true heart of a pastor. I consider Pastor Jon a friend and a mentor, and he's provided some fantastic opportunities for spiritual growth for me and my family, so I felt some conflict when I told him that I wanted to rejoin the band. But I knew I had to do it: I had to clean my slate.

My reasoning was that I had been a sober member of the band for many years, and whoever pulled me off the Megadeth campus for eight years—whether God did it, or I did it, or if it was a combination of the two of us—I was clearly supposed to go back and take care of unfinished business. In Corinthians 6, Jesus says that if you're at a church and you're ready to praise God, but you have anything outstanding with your fellow man, leave the church immediately. Don't give up your money, don't sing any songs. Go and make it right with that other person before you come back into the church and stand there as a hypocrite praising God.

That's pretty heavy, and for me it meant I had to go and repair my relationship with Megadeth. It's interesting to have gone to college to study business and also work in a church, because the church is where business and spirituality come together. Boy, what a collision that can be if it's born of human design.

So what does my future hold? It appears that we can do Megadeth for as long as we want, or at least as long as we can still headbang and fit into our jeans. We'll keep producing new material, and there seems to be an ongoing demand for us to play live. I'm still active as a volunteer with MEGA Life! Someday I'll likely settle down into a church and work there, but until then, an amazing opportunity for some ministry work lies ahead of me. If there's ever a chance to be of service, which happens because people e-mail me from all over the world asking about sobriety, I take it.

I truly have a "mega life." God is the author of all of life and everything fits together perfectly.

A THOUGHT

Faith and Religion

I know I've talked a lot about faith, God, religion, and more in this book. I realize that might seem strange to you, coming from a heavy metal guy. Trust me, it would sound odd to me, too, if I was reading this book. However, we all have our path. Just know that these are my discoveries as they have come to me. Hopefully as the years pass by, I'll have even more new awakenings about such matters.

Although I was raised in a respectable and religious home, I needed to have my own faith journey, rather than simply believe what they told me in Sunday school, or from the pulpit of the Lutheran church as a kid. I'm the kind of guy who learns much better with hands-on training, when my back is against the wall and it's "do or die" time. Faith has been the same for me.

There are probably as many different opinions on faith and religion as there are people who hold them. As for my religion and views of the Bible, I quit going to church after I was confirmed in my Lutheran faith at age sixteen. Even though I've worked on staff in church now for several years, I still think like an unchurched person rather than a regular attendee, because that's my life's walk. Given the choice as a teenager, I walked away, and it never got any better until I was brought to my knees by addiction at the age of twenty-five.

So, to me, the ritual of faith—often known as religion—is not as important as the actual *act* of faith. Scripture reminds us that faith is asking for something we cannot yet see, but acting as if it has already happened. Once we do this enough and see tangible results, it's almost as if we don't even need faith because we then have proof.

My adult church life began after I got clean in 1990. Julie and I attended a few churches in Los Angeles in the early '90s. We were yearning for the word of God in some shape or form. I remember going over to see the famed author Marianne Williamson give her lectures in Santa Monica back in 1992, just before her appearance on Oprah Winfrey's show that propelled her to international fame. Her lectures were based on "A Course in Miracles" teachings, which included Christianity, a dash of New Age ideas, and personal thoughts and inspirations. We drove around listening to her tapes, which helped us cop a good spiritual buzz.

At the same time, we listened to motivational guru Tony Robbins's tapes. I never really got where he was coming from, but it did help Julie quit her job. Maybe it was the right thing at the right time to help her do something she knew she needed to do. She is decisive, and when she has her mind made up, she does it. I'm not as good like that, but have gotten much better in recent years.

Once we had kids, we began a quest for something much more solid. We become our own parents when we have kids, and suddenly all that rebelling we used to do isn't so cool anymore. In fact, once I had kids of my own I realized that my parents were actually pretty hip and had it together—even that church thing.

After we attended a few New Age–type churches following our move to Arizona in 1993, we began regularly attending a modern non-denominational Bible-based church in Scottsdale. During the *Risk* recording, the music leader asked Julie if I'd be up for playing in their band during my spare time at home. I'd been around the God campus long enough to know that this wasn't just a guy asking for a bassist: this was The Man upstairs pointing me to yet another milestone on my faith journey. After I played a few times, they asked me to share my testimony, and things really started to kick into high gear for me and my faith. God has a good sense of humor to know that I will probably attend church more if I can bring my bass with me. He should know—He created me.

A few years later, after Athena was born, we were getting the kids plugged into their preschool, which was at the nearby Lutheran church we had attended once on our arrival in Scottsdale in 1993. We loved the service, but the pastor announced it was his last sermon and that he would be retiring, so we moved on. And yet here we were only a few years later, with kids in tow for preschool. At the urging of our children, we started attending church there, so they could be with their friends. I presented my Lutheran Confirmation credentials and we officially joined as a family.

Although I was fifteen years sober by that time, and had been attending church regularly, the question still lingered: "Is this Jesus stuff real? Did this really happen?" Then a thought hit me one day as we were sitting in the front row of this very church: "You didn't believe in sobriety by way of spirituality, but you finally acted as if it was going to work, and it did." So why shouldn't I apply that same reasoning to my Christian faith? Bingo, that was it. I was on the path and have never looked back.

CHAPTER SIXTEEN

New Frontiers

"Religion is for those afraid of hell, but spirituality is for those
who have already been there."

—Anonymous

My new life started over twenty-three years ago as I write this. What have I learned since then?

For one, I'm definitely not perfect, and please forgive me if I give the impression that I think I am. With that said, my life is really an example that even when we go astray, the good Lord can pick us back up and give us a second chance. We're all human and fall short of perfection, but through our faith in God we can be forgiven. That was really my take on Christianity. God, through our faith in Christ, can not only give us eternal life but also restore us and give us the chance to do things differently the second time around in this lifetime. From there, we are born anew to gain a new understanding and purpose for our lives. In effect, that happened when I offered a prayer to a God I didn't understand back in the fall of 1989. From there, something happened that brought me to where I am today.

I realized a long time ago that I'm either letting God into my life or pushing him out: there is no in-between. That is true with every moment, every decision I make, and every action I take. Once I abide by that, my thoughts eventually start to purify as well.

As they told me in early sobriety, "You can't think your way into right actions. You have to act your way into right thinking." My initial journey into this new life was about letting go of all the stuff that was broken and didn't work. That allowed all the good things that were put into my life as a youngster to come back in and fill me up again.

Perhaps you think that faith isn't relevant to your life. I understand that. After all, when I first journeyed into these new frontiers with all my antagonism toward God, the only one who was holding Him at the door was me. I'm the only one who pushed Him away.

As far as religion goes, I'm very liberal in a lot of ways. Conversely, I might be conservative about money and so on. My liberal beliefs come from traveling the world and seeing it with my own two eyes. It wasn't like one day I was a drug addict and then I woke up a Jesus freak the next day. It simply wasn't like that. It was a process for me.

I still find the religious issues confusing at times and I have had my doubts over the years, too. I don't want you to think that there was a sudden, enveloping experience for me. I'm human, and I know that ultimately I will have doubts and wonder what it would be like to reenter the abyss. I think the best I will ever be on this issue, in this lifetime, is a work in progress.

Will I try to sell you the idea that you must have faith? No. There's a tradition I like to abide by: "Attraction works better than promotion," and it's something I try to adhere to in my life. How we live is a better testimony than running around talking about how spiritual we think we are. It's one of the reasons why I've never really been outwardly vocal about my faith journey in the professional arena of music. In reality, my belief is more "live and let live." I live my life my way and I let you live yours your way, without needing to make you see everything the way I see it.

Everything I've learned about faith that has been effective for me has been instilled in me through getting clean from drugs, and I've made that very clear to the various pastors and churches who have wanted me to step forward and give testimony. They want me to stand up and talk about how the love of Jesus saved me, and all that stuff—but that's not how it happened. I did come back to believe, but it was coming through the wide-open doors of recovery that made it possible.

Kerry King (Slayer): When it comes to religion, I admire anyone—whether I agree with them or not—who doesn't just chime in with, "Well, I believe this, and this is the way everybody in America thinks." I give Ellefson credit for that. He doesn't try to talk me out of my beliefs.

I didn't fall to my knees, pray to Jesus and get saved, and then see a burning bush on a white cloud. For me, the process was much slower, more methodical and intellectual: I came to my belief in a process of spiritual awakening. That's why I didn't just get saved, quit Megadeth, go into the church, and turn my back on it all.

I believe that God kept Megadeth in my life for a reason. He kept my relationship with Dave Mustaine alive for a reason. That which you don't learn from will keep presenting itself until you finally learn its lesson. And to a large degree, my relationship with Dave was something that kept presenting itself until I finally learned the lesson—to step up and be in acceptance of it without trying to change it. We both bring something unique to the table, and we don't have to try to be like each other. Again, live and let live.

When I was younger I was generally a passive, easygoing, path-of-least-resistance kind of guy, and having someone like Dave in my life has been very beneficial to me. He is a very bold, extreme man on the edge, and he really pushed me out there in a lot of ways to my benefit. At the same time, I bring something different, which is caution and a look-before-you-leap approach. The two of us are yin and yang, which is really the spirit and the beauty of Megadeth. Without either of us there is a different dynamic. There are specific roles in this band that were put in place, and I look back at them now with a seasoned sense of sobriety and from a Christian walk.

God has always been with me. I was sixteen years old when my heart said to me, "Go west, young man," and two years later I moved to California. A week after that I met Dave and we started Megadeth. Those things didn't just happen by accident. In light of all the things I've been through, I look back with the benefit of hindsight and I think, "First of all, the good Lord has a sense of humor!" Secondly, it's interesting that He can use something as insane as a rock band as a tool to push out to the front line. Our passions can be used for many purposes in this life, if we are open to seeing the possibilities.

I remember talking to my mother about my faith one day when I turned down the dirt road to our house off Highway 71, which is the main route north of Jackson, Minnesota. I'll never forget saying to her, "I feel really happy; I feel really good about my life and my friends. They like me, I like them, and everything's great."

It was shortly after that time, age fifteen, that I started drinking, which took me on a ten-year journey in the other direction. Once that life got close to me, it started to pull me away from church, and to pull me away from what I call G.O.D., or "Good Orderly Direction." You may ask, if faith allowed me to feel so good about everything, then why did I drink? A good question! I've come to see it as curiosity. Sometimes our curious nature leads us into things we know we shouldn't do, but we do them anyway. From there, often a price must be paid. That's where drugs and alcohol took me.

The simplicity of my journey is that in my darkest hour I reached out to God, and something happened. When I was out of options, He was the last one there for me and then He started to do for me what I couldn't do for myself. I surrendered and reached out to Him, and things started moving quickly in a new direction. This was the pivotal moment for me: it was a spiritual experience. The obsession with using drugs and alcohol began to lift, because when you're strung out, not only do you have a physical addiction, but your head can't get out of the game either. That's what started to happen: I started to get out of the game. I started to find some resolve: I thought, "You know what? Maybe I can actually beat this."

Why, then, was I so prejudiced toward the Church during my drug years? A lot of that was simply because when you're living in darkness, the light is not your friend. When I first met Dave back in 1983, heavy metal was fascinated with Satan. Black Sabbath is an example of music that has a dark, enchanting allure to it, and the late Ronnie James Dio wrote mystical lyrics which, at my age, I found very captivating. When Iron Maiden's *Number of the Beast* album came out, it was pretty much my high school theme song! I've read the Book of Revelation: now I know where Maiden got those lyrics from, and I see that story through different eyes. But because I was drinking and partying, metal lyrics took on a whole different meaning for me back in my younger days.

As I started to go down darker roads, drugs and alcohol pulled me even faster in that direction, and all of a sudden I was a vampire. I really lived vampire hours. I used to brag that I lived "the other nine to five." I started my day at 9 P.M. and went to bed at 5 A.M. So as a result, I was moving away from everything the Church talks about: Good Orderly Direction.

Another reason for my prejudice was that I saw the Church as the establishment. I look back now and I think that most of us musicians are kids from families that probably had some religion in one form or another. I remember that some pastors would come to our church when I was a kid, and they would tell us how evil rock 'n' roll records were, and they would have these big record-burning parties. They burned LPs by Rush and KISS and Judas Priest—all my favorites.

It was such a turnoff. I thought, "If this is what Christianity is about, then forget it!" I knew that KISS wasn't a drug band, they were a fun party band, and I thought that these people were so misinformed. *They* had such a hard-line prejudice against everything that I completely turned away from them. I realized to at least some degree that I was dancing with the dark side myself, even though I wasn't fully in bed with it yet, but to turn back and acknowledge that the religious people were right in any way would have been to show weakness. Or so I thought. But there was always a little thing inside me, hanging on to the church, no matter how bad things got.

For that reason, not taking a drink or a drug is of paramount importance, above all else. There would be nothing for me in that case: no faith, no family, no band, nothing. I had to be convinced of that before I could really embrace a new life. The trick for me is to always remember that. That's why I'm active in faith development. You're either growing toward it or you're going away from it.

I've turned down several gigs because of their association with drugs. A lot of musicians smoke weed, and I don't want to walk around with a contact high. Even though I'm not physically smoking it, I'm breathing in secondhand smoke, and all it takes is a little bit of spiritual sharpness to wear off because there's some pot around me. All of a sudden, that's a way for the enemy to come back in again.

That said, I don't have a problem being around people who are drinking. Sometimes I see someone drinking a beer and I think, "Wow, a beer would taste good," but it doesn't get its hooks into me so that I obsess about it. I don't mind being in a party situation for a while if there's a reason for me to be there, like there's a business conversation or I'm just sharing some camaraderie with a friend. I don't mind being in it for a minute or two for that purpose. But I have to be honest with myself: if my purpose for being there really doesn't exist, and I'm trying to get a little pleasure from the atmosphere, then it's definitely time to leave.

One of the good things about being a seasoned musical artist with some maturity is that you can say no to certain opportunities. You can measure the money, which is obviously a consideration but not the only one, against your spiritual health and well-being. If nothing else, it stems from the desire for self-preservation. Most of the problems that befell me in the 1980s and early '90s were of my own making, out of selfish ambition, lust, greed, and "I need to make a ton of money so I can afford to buy more stuff." I was young, and experience has a way of teaching these lessons.

The struggle in my head going on right before I got clean in early 1990 was that quitting drugs and alcohol would take all the fun out of rock 'n' roll. That was the lie of addiction speaking to me, saying, "Look how great you play when you're on heroin; look how creative it makes you; you're not inhibited; blah blah blah." That's the voice of the enemy. The rush of walking out onstage is still there, as strong as it ever was. Anyone who has ever rehearsed music with a band in a secure environment will know that as soon as you step out onstage, it's an instant adrenaline rush. All theatrical performers of any sort have to be on autopilot to deliver their performance, because if you're actually thinking about your performance, you're missing a big part of the moment.

It's simple. God does for us slowly what the drugs used to do for us quickly. When we put that junk into our bodies, we cut off our route to Him, and in doing so we shortchange ourselves. Some people can party and have a great time: I can't. I've already proven that, so when I see that happening, as much as the first couple of beers and joints look like they're a lot of fun, all I have to do is see people three hours later when they're ten shots of Jäger and five joints into the night, and I think, "Thank God I didn't start out when they started out." I usually go to bed happy, thinking, "What looked good at 9 P.M. doesn't look so good at 1 A.M. . . ."

Here's the bottom line for me. I came back to find faith because of my need to have complete, 100 percent abstinence. I couldn't do a little: I had to do none. I had to stop completely. We have a saying: "If you sober up a horse thief, what do you have? A sober horse thief." At some point, the actual behavior has to change. Once you remove the drugs and alcohol, there's still a spiritual void, and that's what gets filled up through God and the process that eventually led me to finding faith.

I just couldn't stop, and when I stopped on my own I couldn't stay stopped on my own. I needed faith to make it work. As a guitar tech friend of mine told me back in 1989, "Seeking help to get clean is a sign of strength, not weakness." How true! I will admit that just because I chose a spiritual path to fill for me slowly what the dope and booze used to fill quickly doesn't mean that it must be the same for everybody. The whole process has been about accepting one's place in this world and everyone else's place, too.

A final word on alcohol and drugs. I think everyone knows, deep inside of them, if they're in over their heads. They know if they've gone to a bad place and if they're having a hard time coming back. All of us, with or without religious or spiritual convictions, can feel there is a level of honesty inside each of us that is our guiding compass. It can be said that is the voice of God speaking to us, and that is the first step in admitting our plight.

My time away from Megadeth really allowed me to do a lot of things with confidence. It taught me that I'm okay without Megadeth, and that's a good place to be. Job or no job, family or no family, we can and should be happy with where God has placed us and with what He gives us. Simple, but not easy. It's about reliance on God, not people. This allows us to be evenly yoked to those He puts in our path.

As a result of how things have panned out, I have a truly wonderful and blessed life. To have a host of friends around the world, to constantly experience new things and integrate into new cultures on foreign shores is all the result of picking up that bass guitar so many years ago. Being able to use my experiences to help others is a gift more valuable than gold. More than anything, I've learned that no life can be a happy one if we are only here to serve ourselves. Service to others is the grease that makes the wheels go around in this life. Just as important, it's never to late to start anew. What once was doesn't have to control the future, and what is today doesn't have to be what it used to be.

Looking back on it all, God seemingly knew the end of my story before I even understood the beginning.

Selected Discography

A THOUGHT
The music

Music is something that moves people. I felt it when I heard rock 'n' roll on the school bus radio, way back in elementary school. I wanted to capture and continue to create that feeling as a musician, for me and the listener.

With that said, hard rock and heavy metal are in my blood. I love this kind of music; it moves me and motivates me. But I also have a soft side that gets satisfied with acoustic instruments like piano and guitar, too. As a musical artist, I like to use all of the brushes and colors in the palette, not just the heavy ones all the time. That creates dynamics, which is what music really offers, and why it resonates so well with the human soul. We are dynamic creatures, and music helps us relate to things and people who are on our same wavelength.

Music started as a passion for me, and to this day it still is. Some musical settings can really rob you of that passion and leave you empty, even to the point of disliking music altogether. I try to avoid those people and those settings. After all, if music is your gift, anyone who tries to quench that gift is like a thief robbing you of what is rightfully yours to enjoy.

MEGADETH

Killing Is My Business . . . and Business Is Good! (1985)

This was a really raw album. I had great hopes and expectations for this album, but because it was on an indie record label we had little time or money to make it what I had hoped it would become. Fortunately, we got to go back and remix and remaster it in 2001—with proper album artwork, too.

Peace Sells . . . but Who's Buying? (1986)

This was initially recorded for release on our first record label, Combat, but was picked up by Capitol in early 1986. It was remixed and released later that year and Capitol became our home for the next several albums, until 2001. It has a uniquely dark and menacing quality about it.

So Far, So Good . . . So What! (1988)

This was a fun and rowdy album, and the lineup change that preceded it was actually invigorating in some ways. It was the first album on which I started to compose for the band, and it was a great experience to work as a cowriter. I remember there was a massive earthquake in L.A. during the recording of the album, which was absolutely frightening—the first one I had ever experienced. A highlight for me was having Steve Jones of the Sex Pistols come in and record guitar on "Anarchy in the U.K." He had some great stories, and as a fan of the Pistols, I was thrilled that he was playing on our album.

Rust in Peace (1990)

This album was written in the darkest days of my career, as far as lineup changes, management changes, and certainly drug use went. Fortunately, out of the darkness came a new dawn that yielded a powerful lineup with great chemistry and many successful albums to follow. It was also the pinnacle of thrash metal with the Clash of the Titans tours in Europe and the U.S. in 1990 and 1991.

Countdown to Extinction (1992)

This is still one of my favorite Megadeth albums. It was such a great time of brotherhood, with everyone writing together and developing the charisma and personalities within the band. Track after track, the songs really shone, and they still sound timeless to me.

Youthanasia (1994)

This period of the band also brings back good memories for me. There was a strong musical camaraderie within the group, and moving the operation to Arizona helped us escape the pretentious atmosphere of living and working in Los Angeles—a city in many ways the polar opposite of everything we stood for as a group.

Cryptic Writings (1997)

Next to *Countdown*, this was probably the group's most musically invigorating and exciting album for me. There was a new optimism in the band, and new management that was very focused on helping carve out a new future for us. It was also the first record we recorded in Nashville, where there was a real buzz because country music was exploding at that time. Ironically, we gained great respect from the town and its notoriously accomplished musicians. I think this was because of our own musical fortitude and the integrity of working with Dann Huff, who had an amazing reputation industrywide with his own guitar playing and producing ventures. The mid- to late 1990s were not very favorable to thrash metal, but this album really thrived and put the band on top in the U.S. in spite of the many obstacles that plagued many of our thrash metal contemporaries. We ended up touring for almost two years on this album as a result.

Risk (1999)

We had just come off of a hugely successful tour with *Cryptic Writings*, and optimism was initially quite high for this next album. However, it was a transitional period for metal music. "Prince of Darkness" is still one of my favorites from this album.

The World Needs a Hero (2001)

This album had a good "band" vibe. Some of my favorite songs are the riff-heavy ones like "Dread and Fugitive Mind" and "Motopsycho," whose video was filmed at the Hells Angels' old haunts in Simi Valley, California. This album was supposed to be our last for Capitol, but instead it became our first album for Sanctuary. Instead, Capitol agreed to release a greatest-hits record called *Capitol Punishment*, which allowed us to move on to our new label. We are one of only a handful of metal bands who actually completed a multiple-album record contract for a major label. It also yielded the double live CD and DVD *Rude Awakening*, which was my last recording with the band until I rejoined in 2010.

Thirteen (2011)

This was my first studio album back with the band after rejoining the fold in 2010. In some ways, it was probably the most fun album I have ever made with Megadeth. The vibes were good and because we had such a limited time to record, with huge tours to follow, there was a real commitment from everyone to make a crushing album and get it completed on schedule. That urgency has made it one of my favorite albums to date.

Super Collider (2013)

This album marks my second record back with Megadeth since 2010. In many ways, it reminds me of some of our albums in the 1990s, mostly because the lineup has been solidified for two albums and extensive world touring. Being on the road tightens up a band, and I think you can hear that chemistry in the tracks of this album.

. . . AND SOME OF MY OTHER BANDS AND RECORDS . . .

F5, *A Drug for All Seasons* (2005), *The Reckoning* (2008)

After Megadeth disbanded in 2002 I had no intention of ever putting another band together in my lifetime. However, after several producing and songwriting opportunities that year, F5 formed in 2003. The band was a refreshing change for me. It was actually one of the most invigorating periods of my life, in terms of opening the floodgates to my songwriting.

Killing Machine (2006)

This opportunity came to me initially through drummer John Dette and vocalist James Rivera. I knew James from his Helstar days, as they opened for Megadeth in the 1980s and I produced an EP for them in 1993. I loved the songs on this album and the band had a great recording lineup. This also included Juan Garcia, whom I had known from 1983, when he was in a band called Abattoir. He played some of the first Megadeth shows in San Francisco in 1984. We never toured this band, as it was mostly an album project with veteran metal musicians.

Temple of Brutality, *Lethal Agenda* (2006)

Peter Scheithauer was the writer of the Killing Machine material, but before we recorded that album he wanted to do a Temple of Brutality record. I think Peter felt that ToB was more thrash metal in style, and a better fit in that era's metal scene. Once we got in the studio to record in Fort Myers, Florida, we had a total blast together and couldn't wait to get the band out on the road. We did some touring the following year and the group was ferocious live, with a great thrash and punk attitude.

Avian, *From the Depths of Time* (2005)

Avian started in 2003 when I produced a song for writer Yan Leviathan at the Saltmine Studios in Mesa, Arizona, close to my home.

From there, Yan got excited about completing a full-length album. So I helped him produce it, brought in most of the musicians, and played bass on the album for him. It also led to a working relationship with former Balance of Power vocalist Lance King, who sang on the album and was able to help with its production once I got busy with F5 the following year.

Acknowledgments

HEARTFELT THANK-YOUS GO OUT TO:

God; my mother, Frances Ellefson, and my brother, Eliot Ellefson; my wife, Julie, and my children, Roman and Athena Ellefson; John and Lucille Foley and the entire Foley family; and all the folks who kindly contributed their stories and editorials to this book, including Frank Bello, Pastor Jon Bjorgaard, Randy Blythe, Chris Broderick, Rex Brown, Alice Cooper, Shawn Drover, Marty Friedman, Greg Handevidt, Glenn Hughes, Scott Ian, Kerry King, Fred Kowalo, Mike Kroeger, Ron Laffitte, Dave McRobb, Chris Poland, Jesse Reeves, and Jay Reynolds.

Mark Abbattista, Mark Adelman, Bruce Adolph, Steve Bailey, Tony Bass, Jim Beaugez, Chuck Behler, Karl Bergstrom, Ray Berry, Ron Bienstock, Scott Bird, Kyle Borman, Paul and Susan Brandt, Corey Brennan, Jim Brennan, Greg Carlson, Jim Carroccio, Jeff Cary, Frank Casanova, Max and Gloria Cavalera, Mike Clink, Bryan Coleman, Steve Conley, John Dallmus and family, John Davis, Jimmy DeGrasso, Jeremy DePena, Ryan Downey, Doug Dreyer, Tamra Feldman, the Fiala family, Paul Fisher, David Fishof, Jonathan Foster, Brett Fredrickson, Ethan Frier, Mike Gaube, Willie Gee, Tom Gibbons, Jerry Giefer, Brent

Giese, Bob Goheen, Larry Hartke, Byron Hontas, Stet Howland, Mark Hudson, John Jackson, Jimmy Jacobs, Val Janes, Jaison John, Angie and Al Jourgensen, Matt Kees, Randy Kertz, Andreas Kisser, Mike LaTronico, Bill Leigh, Troy Lucketta, Kirk Martin, Larry Mazer, Brian McDonald, Lee Meecham, Mark Menghi, Nick Menza, Tony Moscal, the Neuenschwander family, Daryl "Barney" Olson, Tim "Ripper" Owens, Al Pitrelli, Keith Rawls, Jon Rayvid, Mike Renault, Pat Ritchie, Jon Romanowski, Peter Scheithauer, Brad Schmidt, Jim Schmidt, the Sether family, Rob Shay, Doug Short, Rat Skates, Mark Slaughter, Dave Small, Rod Smallwood, Billy Smiley, Andy Somers, Michael Spriggs, Dale Steele, Fran Strine, Doug Thaler, Scott Uchida, Mr. Udo, Jon Vesley, Randy Walker, Jeff Waters, Todd Weber, Mary Ann Werner and her family, Scott Wesley Brown, Jason Witte, Steve Wood, Bill Xavier, Jeff Yonker, Jeff Young, Danny Zelisko.

Dr. Wollenberg and all at Concordia Seminary, Shepherd of the Desert Lutheran Church and School, the Christian Musician Summit, all the teachers and staff of the Jackson, Minnesota, school system, CCV, the friends of Bill W. worldwide.

Bass Guitar Magazine, Bass Player magazine, Beamz Interactive, EMG, ETA, Hartke, Jackson Guitars, Jim Dunlop, NSFC, Peavey Electronics, Peterson Tuners, Planet Waves, Shure, SIT Strings.

Anthrax, Guns N' Roses, Iron Maiden, Motörhead, Metallica, Nickelback, Slayer, Slipknot.

ADDITIONAL THANKS GO OUT TO:

My agent, Lisa Gallagher; Matthew Hamilton; Joel McIver; Philis Boultinghouse; and everyone at Howard Books for believing.

Dave Mustaine, for all the years of musical brotherhood.

In memory of my father, Gordon G. Ellefson; Craig S.; and Gar Samuelson.

Index